Judith McCall.   £30-00

THE CAUTIOUS EXPERT

THE CAUTIOUS EXPERT

A social analysis of developments in the practice of educational psychology

J. C. QUICKE

Lecturer in the Division of Education,
University of Sheffield

THE OPEN UNIVERSITY PRESS
Milton Keynes

The Open University Press
A division of
Open University Educational Enterprises Limited
12 Cofferidge Close
Stony Stratford
Milton Keynes MK11 1BY, England

First published 1982

Copyright © 1982 The Open University Press

All rights reserved. No part of this work
may be reproduced in any form, by
mimeograph or by any other means,
without permission in writing from
the publisher.

British Library Cataloguing in Publication Data

Quicke, J.C.
   The cautious expert: a social analysis of
   developments in the practice of educational
   psychology.
   1. Educational psychology
   I. Title
   370.15   LB1051

ISBN 0   335   10110   0

Printed in Great Britain at the Alden Press,
Oxford, London and Northampton

Contents

	Introduction	vii
1	The establishment of educational psychology	1
2	The emerging profession: post-war developments	20
3	Phychometrics, professional survival and the traditional practitioner paradigm	40
4	Knowledge in practice: a questionnaire and interview study	59
5	The non-directive style	86
6	The behavioural approach	106
7	Sociological and radical alternatives	122
	Appendix 1 Letter to educational psychologists	151
	Appendix 2 The questionnaire on professional knowledge	152
	Appendix 3 Questionnaire results	156
	References	161
Unpublished Documents		169
Index		171

Acknowledgements

Acknowledgements are due to all those colleagues, friends and students who, through discussing their ideas with me, have helped me to develop my own thinking. In particular, I should like to thank those educational psychologists without whose co-operation the empirical study would have been impossible. For obvious reasons they have to remain anonymous. Thanks must also be expressed to Julie Brayford for her careful typing of part of the manuscript. I also owe thanks to my wife, Anne, who, in addition to typing some chapters, has had to put up with me when my energies have been devoted to writing.

Introduction

In recent years, the practice of educational psychology by educational psychologists (EPs) working in local authority School Psychological Services has allegedly been in a state of change. Within the profession, there has been a growing dissatisfaction with what has been referred to as the 'traditional model'. The critique of intelligence testing and psychometrics has been but one aspect of this. Other criticisms have been more general regarding psychometrics as part of a model of practice which has more in common with medicine than psychology or education: a model which uses the language of medicine — 'diagnosis', 'abnormal', 'treatment' — and results in children being given a 'sick' label like disturbed or subnormal. Still other criticisms have focused on the kinds of explanations provided by psychology. These explanations, it is claimed, have emphasized biologically-oriented 'within child' factors rather than social factors, and have thus tended to play down the role of the school. Further criticisms have referred to the role style of the EP — as a visiting 'scientific' expert — which has been seen as an anachronism in an age of teamwork and dialogue, as well as being founded on the false assumption that educational psychology is, somehow, a 'neutral', value-free science. Related to this is another criticism which sees the EP as a 'bureaucratized professional' having to work to order in the local educational authority and applying only that aspect of his knowledge which fits this role.

Outside the profession also there have been questions asked about the role of the EP. These have sometimes resulted in contradictory pressures on him.* On the one hand, there are those,

* the male pronoun is used as a literary convention only and no sex bias is intended.

mainly teachers, who have criticized EPs for being so preoccupied with 'scientific' assessment procedures that they have neglected to provide practical hints for teachers about what to actually do in the classroom to help the 'problem child'. On the other hand, there are those, mainly administrators, who fail to see why EPs should be so wary about seeing individual children or administering IQ tests in relation to the selection of children for special education.

To some extent these questions and criticisms can be related to more general changes both inside and outside the profession. EPs, like other professionals, have had to become more accountable in the present political and economic climate. There has been more concern in the Warnock era for the integration of the 'handicapped', and this has necessitated an expansion of the EPs' advisory role. The position of the profession has also changed. By the mid 1970s the profession had 'come of age' and acquired quasi-legal, official status in relation to the assessment and disposal of children with special educational needs.

Different EPs have responded differently to the changing circumstances. Although there is much common ground, one's superficial impression is of considerable variation across the country. Some school psychological services are still mainly traditionally oriented, others are attempting to develop alternative models. Even within the same school psychological service, there may be differing persepectives on change, sometimes leading to inconsistencies in the overall impact of the team of psychologists. Consumers of psychological services might well be forgiven for not knowing what to expect of their local EP.

The main aim of this book is to provide an up to date account and clarification of the 'state of play' with respect to the tension between status quo maintaining and change oriented practices. There is a great deal of confusion both within and outside the profession about the nature and extent of changes. We do not know if it is a minority or a majority who have largely abandoned traditional activities such as intelligence testing. We do not know just how popular alternative approaches are, or whether or not all 'alternatives' are the radical break with tradition they claim to be. We do not know what kinds of knowledge present day EPs are using in their practices and how this differs from that of their predecessors. And there is very little information on how EPs themselves perceive the direction of change.

In chapter 1 an historical base line is provided for the ensuing discussion. This chapter is concerned with the 'roots' of traditional practice. It describes how 'modern educational psychology' became established, and the role it played in education. The profession of educational psychologist is introduced and the early role of child guidance clinics and school psychological services described. Chapter 2 provides further material on the development of the profession which, hopefully, sheds light on its attitude to change, while Chapter 3 looks at the 'staple diet' of psychometrics and intelligence testing, and assesses the function of this for professional identity and its contribution to current practices. By the end of this chapter the reader should have a clear idea of the nature of what is described as the 'traditional practitioner paradigm', and the nature of the profession with which it is identified.

Chapter 4 describes a two-part, empirical study. The first part involved asking EPs working in local education authorities to complete a questionnaire about their professional knowledge. The second was an interview study involving a small number of EPs in one local authority. The study was designed to answer the question: are most EPs still working within the limits of the traditional paradigm, and what indications are there of alternative approaches being adopted?

Chapters 5, 6 and 7 contain a discussion and evaluation of a number of approaches which purport to be radically different from practices under the umbrella of the traditional practitioner paradigm. Chapter 5 looks at the 'non-directive style' which is a general approach to practice based on models of the person which, unlike the determinist models of the traditional paradigm, emphasize the relative autonomy of the individual and the importance of studying subjectivity. Chapter 6 looks at the 'behavioural approach' which attempts to provide an alternative perspective on assessment and remediation. Both these approaches allegedly differ from traditional practice by forcing the EP to go into the classroom where the action is. Interpretations of the questionnaire and interview study suggest they are both relatively popular among practitioners. Not so popular are the sociologically-oriented approaches based on 'systems analysis' and the 'interactionist perspective'. These are dealt with in the first part of Chapter 7.

Chapter 7 also includes some possible outlines for a radical practice. In a sense, the whole book can be conceived of as a 'ground clearing exercise' for these final recommendations. It is always easier to criticize than to create and this chapter contains no more than a number of tentative suggestions as to possible strategies. It is a chapter, therefore, which is by no means concluded.

In addition to the main aim of clarifying and evaluating

different practices, there are two subsidiary aims or themes which relate to certain omissions within the conventional literature on the profession. First, although there have been several straightforward descriptions of the work of school psychological services, there have been few that have been appreciative of the various dilemmas faced by EPs in their day to day practice. Psychologists are people too! Like all of us, they have doubts and identity problems and develop strategies for coping with a demanding environmet. One subsidiary aim, then, is to present a sympathetic account of the psychology of psychologists. It may be felt that to 'reveal all' in this way (as in the interview study, for example) does a disservice to the profession, but I would argue that such information helps to break down barriers between occupational groups, facilitates communication and ultimately enhances rather than undermines mutual respect.

The second subsidiary aim is to provide a text on the practice of educational psychology which does not duck theoretical issues. Most conventional texts are guilty of this. The knowledge resources that EPs draw upon are listed and briefly described but there is little evaluation of the worthiness of their conceptual bases. It is in order to encourage an awareness of the theoretical issues 'behind' practices that I have concentrated in some chapters on an explication and critique of some influential theories. There is, of course, a risk here of becoming too abstract and academic, but I have tried to avoid this by choosing theories, e.g., George Kelly's personal construct theory (see Chapter 6), which are relatively popular and have an immediate relevance for practitioners. It is only by being sensitive to theoretical issues that the EP can reflect in an intellectually serious way on the rationale of his practice. If he is concerned with change then such reflection is indispensable.

CHAPTER 1

The establishment of educational psychology

An important part of the professional identity of educational psychologists and thus of their special contribution is their acquaintance with a body of knowledge rooted in an academic discipline. Several authors have noted the importance of the knowledge base as a distinguishing feature of professionals. Heraud (1970) states that: 'A major condition for the distinction between professional and non-professional is the possession of knowledge and skill which is not generally available'.

Of course, such knowledge is not the only knowledge resource educational psychologists draw upon in their day to day decision making. As Valett (1963) points out, 'cultural background' and 'practical experience' also contribute to the theoretical framework. But, nevertheless, there is a sense in which certain aspects of their knowledge are more 'fundamental', i.e., knowledge derived from 'education in the various schools of thought pertaining to human behaviour and mental functioning' (page 24).

The second crucial aspect of the educational psychologists' identity is their employment by the State. They have been traditionally located in local authority education departments and their general function has been to assist the authority to carry out its duties with respect to the various Education Acts. Although their role has included a wide range of activities, in most authorities they have been located for the most part in a service closely bound up with special education structures. They have played a major role in the diagnosis, assessment and treatment of children with special educational needs.

In this chapter the development of the knowledge base — modern educational psychology — is traced from its beginnings in the nineteenth century to its establishment in the first few decades of the twentieth century. This is followed by a description of the educational context and special structures in which the educational psychologist operated in the pre-Second World War period.

THE RISE OF THE 'NEW' PSYCHOLOGY

The 'new' psychology on which modern educational psychology was founded was certainly different from the 'old' psychology with respect to its presuppositions and methodology, but not unique in its application to education. It is often forgotten that before they became exhausted by the end of the nineteenth century the 'old' psychological ideas did have a part to play in education and were influential in schools. Faculty psychology, for example, gave support to the idea of formal systematic training of the powers of the mind which was dominant in the training colleges in the nineteenth century. Critics of the old psychology questioned its empirical basis, and its subservience to philosophy from which it was not distinguished as a separate discipline. They also questioned the formal and mechanical approach to teaching that it gave rise to.

How did the new psychology contrast with the old? Put simply, it was a psychology influenced by the developments in the natural sciences of biology and genetics, and more concerned with experimentation, observation and individual differences. Man and child were conceived more dynamically as active, purposive organisms interacting with an ever-changing environment. Not that there was any sharp break between the old and the new. There were many transitional figures who, like James Sully and James Ward, could be regarded as the founding fathers of modern psychology but who were initially rooted in the old psychology.

If one man can be said to be the first representative of the new psychology, particularly in relation to education in Britain, it is probably William McDougall. A Darwinian, he produced a thesis in his book *An Introduction to Social Psychology* (1908) which demonstrated how man's psychological and social life sprang from the instincts which were provided by natural selection. Many psychologists and educationalists who were influential in the British scene have acknowledged a debt to McDougall: C. Burt, R. Rusk, G. Thompson and P. Nunn, to name but four. When W. D. Wall (1956) wrote that 'From the outset, British educational psychology emphasised social factors...' (page 79), he was recognizing the significance of McDougall's contribution, although underplaying the biologically reductionist aspects of his model.

The basic message of the new psychology was that education should take into account the biological, genetic and psychological realities of child development. To some extent education had always done this but there had been a tendency for children to be treated uniformly, as if individual differences were of little significance. The new psychology, however, provided incontrovertible evidence of the nature of these differences. The evidence was derived from studies of an 'objective' and 'scientific' kind.

THE NEW PSYCHOLOGY APPLIED TO EDUCATION

From the early years of the twentieth century, the interaction between this psychology and education became an important feature of the educational scene in Britain as in other parts of Europe. Hearnshaw (1964) points to three institutions — the universities, local and national State authorities and voluntary bodies — which were important in mediating psychology to schools and assisting it to become established as arguably the most important theoretical resource for education. It was the Board of Education who as early as 1899 included texts by Bain and Sully in the Syllabus for the Training of Teachers and who at various times between the wars produced documents and reports heavily influenced by current developments in psychological science, for example, 'Psychological Tests of Educable Capacity' (1924) and 'The Primary School' (1935). At local level, the London County Council, successor to the progressive London School Board, inherited the services of three psychologically oriented inspectors — Ballard, Kimmins and Winch. P. B. Ballard (1865-1950) did work on memory and drew attention to the phenomenon of 'reminiscence'. Later he became interested in speech problems, but his most famous contribution was probably his book *Group Tests of Intelligence* published in 1922 which was extremely popular with teachers and went through several editions. He was a contributor to the *Journal of Experimental Pedagogy* which later became the *British Journal of Educational Psychology*. W. H. Winch (1864-1935) was also interested in memory, particularly transfer effects, and contributed to influential journals like that of the Child Study Movement (to be discussed later). C. W. Kimmins (1865-1948) produced several books on psychology. These inspectors had attended courses at the New Education Department at University

College (started by Sully) and were responsible for Burt's appointment as the first local authority psychologist in 1913.

Relative to other countries, psychology was slow to become established in British universities. C. S. Myers was appointed in 1906 as the first lecturer in Experimental Psychology at Cambridge, and developments at Oxford were even later. It was not until 1936 that a small Institute of Experimental Psychology was established at the University. By 1939 there were only six chairs in Psychology — three in London and one at each of Cambridge, Oxford and Manchester. The total number of lecturing staff was thirty.

According to Stewart (1972) the study of education in universities in England and Wales had been in existence virtually since the beginning of the century. The establishment of the Day Training Colleges in universities in the 1890s helped to secure a university status for education. The importance of this was acknowledged by Dent (1977):

> One can hardly exaggerate the importance of the introduction of the day training colleges. They increased substantially the supply of trained teachers for Public Elementary schools, ended the isolation of the training colleges and the near-monopoly of teacher training by religious denominations, gave the study of education academic status and raised the prestige of the Elementary school teacher. (p 33)

Many of the staff of these colleges were influenced by the new psychology and wrote books for educationalists which popularized the findings of psychological research. Two outstanding figures at the London Day Training College were Sir John Adams and Sir Percy Nunn, the latter succeeding the former as Principal in 1922. Nunn's famous book *Education, its Data and First Principles* (1920) showed the influence of McDougall's social psychology as well as a number of other perspectives such as psychoanalysis (which was becoming popular at that time in Britain) and Dewey's theories. According to Tibble (1961) Nunn's book was written at a time when the doctrine of instincts was at its peak: 'In the next twenty years, criticisms of the doctrine particularly from the behaviourist but also implicit in the findings of cultural anthropology rose to a crescendo' (p 68).

An important figure in Scotland was R. R. Rusk who became Director of the Scottish Council of Education Research in 1928. He was critical of the vagueness and methodology of the Child Study Movement and laid out his criticisms in his book *Experimental Education* (1929) which was arguably the first book on education psychology as it is known today. According to Rusk this subject was not merely applied psychology but without doubt an independent study and a discipline in its own right. The contents of his book give an indication of the range of topics covered: sensory acuity and discrimination, types of observation, forms of memory, the nature of the child's mental imagery and thinking, quantitative estimates of general intelligence, suggestibility, individual differences, the importance of different endowments, statistics, attention and perception. Although 'techniques of learning' are mentioned, no use is made of Watsonian behaviourism or Thorndike.

A second book which exemplified the emergence of educational psychology as we know it today was that of Godfrey Thomson who took up his chair at the Moray House Training College in 1925. His *Instinct, Intelligence and Character* was published in 1924. The particular significance of this book is that although it is typically British in combining instinct theory with a factor analytic theory of intelligence, the influence of American behaviourism is not inconsiderable.

In the provincial universities, many of the early professors of education were enthusiastic advocates and popularizers of psychology applied to education. In Birmingham, C. W. Valentine (1919–46) was the first of a number of professors of education — he was followed by F. J. Schonell and E. A. Peel — with this orientation.

THE ROLE OF PSYCHOLOGY IN EDUCATION

For the pioneers, who established educational psychology as an independent discipline, the question of the role of psychology in education would have been relatively easy to answer. Psychology was a progressive force because it was part and parcel of scientific progress. Education could only be improved by educationalists becoming aware of the child as an individual and of the need to foster that individuality. Children's social, intellectual and emotional potential needed to be realized, and psychological knowledge provided the conceptual tools for the achievement of this.

Looked at in this way, the only problem on the horizon was not a theoretical but a practical one: how best to deliver this psychology to schools. Thus there was a great need for popular texts for teachers and it was important for training colleges to think hard about how to incorporate psychology into their syllabuses. It was also necessary to establish machinery which could facilitate the spread of ideas from one section of education to another. The creation of Institutes of Education (like the one at the University of London in 1932) representing the close association that was growing up between teachers, training colleges, universities and local education authorities did much to assist the dissemination of psychology.

However, there are alternative interpretations which suggest that the consequences of applying psychology to education were not all sweetness and light. The issues here are complex and really deserve more space than can be given in this introduction, but at the very least one should point out that the influence of psychology was decidedly ambiguous. Much depended on which aspects of 'modern educational psychology' were highlighted and how they were interpreted and used by policy makers. At the risk of oversimplifying, one can distinguish between what might be described figuratively as the 'dynamic' and 'static' aspects of the subject which were variously linked with either progressive and radical or regressive and reactionary educational ideologies and practices. An example of a 'static' aspect might be psychometrics.

The role of psychometrics

The great popularizers, Adams, Rusk and Valentine, all interpreted the work of the psychometrically-oriented psychologists. Tests became more and more sophisticated throughout the twentieth century. The invention of the correlation coefficient represented a particularly significant step forward. It was originally the idea of Karl Pearson but as developed by Fisher, a Cambridge mathematician, it made a great contribution to experimental pedagogy. Further advances were made by Spearman between 1911 and 1913. The other giant in this field was Thompson who together with Burt in 1947 founded the *Journal of Statistical Psychology*. These developments percolated through to education through the work of men like Ballard and Burt both of whom produced large numbers of tests for use in schools.

Psychometrics was a technology that enabled a psychologist to produce standardized measures of psychological characteristics and one of its main uses in the education system was in the assessment of educational abilities and attainments. Although there was disagreement among psychologists and psychometricians about the interpretation of various statistical data, their views were consistent enough to make a profound impact on the deliberations of the various consultative committees — Hadow, Spens and, to a lesser extent, Norwood — whose recommendations were eventually incorporated in legislation which shaped the structure of education in the post-war period.

It was the psychologists' claim to be able to differentiate children scientifically that was so appealing to administrators and policy makers. Not only was it possible to measure innate ability objectively, but group tests could be produced which permitted large numbers of children to be assessed with relative ease. Using this tool, it was possible to predict the educational achievement of children and thus to legitimize a system of streaming in the elementary schools.

It is difficult to do justice to the politics of educational reform in this period in a brief space, but a reasonable interpretation is that Hadow reorganization had the effect of maintaining the pyramidal structure of education required by a hierarchically organized society and this was not unintended by some powerful people in the Board of Education. Some of the leading figures of the day were quite open about their élitism and would have agreed with the views of one of the principal architects of the Balfour Act (1902), Sir Robert Morant, that the majority of children should be educated according to the class to which they belonged and would continue to belong. As Simon (1974) points out, many of the more progressive aspects of the original Hadow report — a concern for aptitudes and interests rather than the narrow concept of ability, the core curriculum, new forms of secondary education for all — were gradually underplayed throughout the period, and eventually ignored. Instead, the emphasis was on treating elementary education as essentially a form of selective machinery for 'proper' secondary education. Streaming was justified in terms of individual needs, but produced a system which excluded the majority of children from receiving a curriculum which would enable them to pass the scholarship and proceed to higher levels. In this way, selection by elimination rather than for differentiation was to become the most important aim of the elementary school, and the psychologists of the period were certainly in part responsible for this turn of events. Just how responsible is difficult to estimate. The conventional view, particularly among psychologists themselves, was that their ideas were to some extent distorted by popularizers and policy makers who had no inhibitions about making somewhat less than cautious and oversimplified assertions about intelligence and intelligence testing. There is undoubtedly some truth in this, but, if so, it should be remembered that some of the popularizers were themselves psychologists and very important and influential ones at that.

Simon (1974) provides the following example:

> In a popular exposition of the new 'science' of mental testing in 1933, to a radio audience, Cyril Burt outlined the conclusions arrived at about the functioning of the human mind. It was a simple, clear straightforward statement admitting no doubts, inviting no argument. By intelligence the psychologist understands inborn, all round intellectual ability. It is inherited, or at least innate, not due to teaching or training; it is intellectual not emotional or moral, and remains uninfluenced by industry or zeal; it is general, not specific, i.e. it is not limited to any particular kind of work, but enters into all we do or say or think. Of all our mental qualities, it is the most far reaching. Fortunately it can be measured with accuracy and ease. (page 241)

The emphasis on measurement, on innate factors, on the intellectual as opposed to other qualities, on the unimportance of the environment reflects only some aspects of the new psychology and omits many others which Burt himself on occasion would have included: the purposive, goal-seeking organism interacting with an environment; the importance of consciousness and experience; the importance of looking at the child as a whole, etc. Psychometry permitted children to be placed in categories in which their educational identities became fixed and from which it was difficult to escape.

Psychology and radical education

If the alliance between psychometry and 'élitist' and 'traditional' educational ideologies and policies was to be expected in view of the narrow, static approach of the former, then one might also expect that the more dynamic aspects of the new psychology would appeal to the more radically inclined. The ideals on which radical education was based were, superficially at any rate, much more in line with the new psychology considered as a whole. In fact, according to Hearnshaw (1964), new ideals in education in the early twentieth century were partly inspired by and in the public mind closely identified with psychology. These ideals were rooted in a belief in 'natural processes'. They implied a child-centred education where there was freedom from restraint, an emphasis on self activity, a recognition of the importance of play and discovery methods and a role for the teacher as a facilitator rather than disciplinarian or curriculum director. Initially at the edges of the system, expressed in the work of Froebel, Montessori and MacMillan in nursery education and pioneers like Homer Lane,

Neill, Russell and Isaacs in experimental schooling, they gradually, throughout the twentieth century, became more influential in the mainstream of education.

One of the leading exponents of these ideals, and one who exemplified the link between them and psychology both in theory and practice, was Susan Isaacs. She was without question a psychologist by profession, although she had also trained as a philosopher. Even when involved in the day to day activities of teaching at Maltinghouse School, she maintained here research orientation and interest in psychological theories. Her work at the school was derived from principles based on a personal synthesis of the theories of Dewey, Montessori and Freud. By the time she took up her appointment as Head of the Department of Child Development at the University of London Institute of Education in 1933 she was respected as an academic and a psychologist as well as an educational practitioner.

Apart from providing interpretations of child nature which 'fed into' the new child-centred education, psychology also acted as something of a restraining force. Psychology may have sprung from the same cultural ethos as progressivism but its particular contribution was its scientific approach to child study. Although Isaacs believed that the child should be the 'centre of gravity' of the teaching–learning process, she was not in favour of total permissiveness and felt that some repression was essential for healthy development. In other words, she was not carried away by the moral imperatives of radical movements, but saw the need to ground the ideals in the alleged psycho-biological realities of child development. Percy Nunn was another liberal thinker and an ally of progressive education, who gave theoretical depth to the movement by his insistence in his book *Education, its Data and First Principles* (1920) on the need for education to be psychologically and 'scientifically' as well as philosophically based. Later in the century, psychologists like Bruner, while accepting the importance of looking at the child as a spontaneous, active learner, showed how teacher intervention was not incompatible with this. By intervening to widen the pupils' horizons and teaching general principles, the child's spontaneity and independence would be enhanced rather than reduced. Thus, there appears to be some truth in the notion that the new psychology served to temper some of the more 'extreme' ideas of the progressive movement, although to what extent this would have happened anyway as a result of the experience of practical application it is impossible to say.

If psychology's role in education is more complex and more

ambiguous than conventional accounts would suggest, then this is something that has to be taken seriously when considering interpretations of the day to day work of educational psychologists. Too often the emphasis has been on the technical aspects of the role with no attempt to analyse the conflicting currents of thought about the nature and status of the knowledge base. The reasons for this underplaying of conflict and glossing over of ambiguity will be discussed in a later chapter. In this chapter, the aim has been to introduce rather than fully explore the problematic of the role of psychology in education.

THE DEVELOPMENT OF SPECIAL EDUCATION

Paralleling the growing interest in psychology applied to general education was the development of services within local authorities which could assist those authorities to carry out their tasks in accordance with the provisions of the various Education Acts. The establishment of universal education provision (Forster's Education Act, [1870], and later Acts which made education compulsory) meant that a variety of needs which previously had remained hidden became increasingly visible. Even when the routine of having to attend school was eventually established (and, of course, non-attendance is still a problem) the children who turned up presented the authorities with a whole host of problems. Sutherland (1981) comments on the fact that the London School Board Committee in 1889 estimated that one child in eight was underfed and suffering from malnutrition, diseases and various disabilities. It was soon recognized that many of these children would have difficulty in coping with normal schooling even when they were fed. The Report of the Royal Commission (1889) (whose terms of reference were extended to include 'special' cases and the deaf in addition to the blind) represented the first official recognition of the necessity for extra or special provision for certain groups of children whose needs could not be met in the ordinary school. The Egerton Commission were no doubt influenced by the complaints of teachers of being 'overpressured', but as Tomlinson (1981) points out there was also an economic motive involved in that it was thought that if such children remained uneducated they would only swell the ranks of the poor. The commission recommended that 'feebleminded' children should be separated for instruction and that 'imbeciles' should be given residential training. It is important to note that this Commission included several medical men, one of whom, Dr Warner, established claims for a special medical competence in detecting feeblemindedness from physical symptoms.

The first local authority special schools for special instruction were founded in London in the 1890s and children were selected on the basis of assessment by the London School Board's medical officer, school inspectors and heads of special schools. However, there was little compulsion from central Government during this period and most of these local authority developments were *ad hoc*. Even the 1899 Elementary Education (Defective and Epileptic Children) Act only allowed rather than required local authorities to create special schools and classes for those with mental defect who were incapable of benefiting from education in normal schools. The consequence of this permissive legislation was that developments were uneven. By 1903, there was some special provision for the mentally defective in London and fifty other authorities.

The influence of the medical profession in these developments was again apparent. In addition to the school boards, it was pressure from medically dominated charitable organizations that led to the setting up of the Committee on Defective and Epileptic Children, many of whose recommendations of 1898 were incorporated in the 1899 Act. The medical witnesses to the Committee stated their opinion that the task of discriminating between imbeciles and feebleminded or defective and defective and normal children was largely a medical one, although they admitted that teachers' opinions should be sought and that inspectors should be involved in the initial phase of selection.

Medical opinion was to continue to hold sway a few years later in 1904 when the Royal Commission on the Care and Control of the Feebleminded commenced its deliberations. Its report in 1908 recommended that the 1899 Act should be amended so that mentally defective children should be the statutary responsibility of Mental Deficiency Committees. As Tomlinson (1981) points out:

> The recommendations of the Royal Commission represented the high point of medical domination of the procedures for assessing defective children. If the care of all defective children had indeed passed to the Board of Control a whole new medically dominated bureaucracy would have developed with far reaching consequences for the education of all subnormal children. (p. 40)

As it was the Mental Deficiency Act of 1913 did not incorporate all the Commission's recommendations. Many of the powers of local authorities under the 1899 Act were retained and when provision of special education under the 1914 Act was made compulsory this strengthened the hand of the local authorities. They were obliged to ascertain children between seven and sixteen years of age who were defective and of these only those who were considered incapable of education in the ordinary school were forwarded to the local Mental Deficiency Committees.

Many of these developments were brought to a halt by the First World War and economic slump. When the Wood Committee (1929) carried out its comprehensive survey it found that many defective children remained unascertained and of those ascertained many were not being catered for in special schools or classes. Although this Committee was set up in 1924 under the auspices of the chief medical officer to the Board of Education, the role of educational psychologists was advanced by the inclusion of Cyril Burt, the LCC psychologist. The influence of psychology was apparent throughout the report, particularly in relation to the diagnosis and assessment of defective functioning, where intelligence tests came to the fore. The importance of these tests was even accepted by the medical profession, and thus the special contribution of psychology was recognized, even though the administration of tests like the Binet was not considered the preserve of educational psychologists.

Wood recommended that those children with IQs between 50 and 70 should be joined with those between 70 and 80 to form a new group known as the 'retarded' who should be given special consideration within the framework of the school system. A single system of special education was proposed for this group which was to be 'brought in to closer relation with the Public Elementary School System and presented to parents not as something both distinct and humiliating but as a helpful variation of the ordinary school'.

There were similar recommendations in relation to sensory handicap in the inter-war years. In 1934, the Board of Education Committee of Inquiry into Problems Relating to Partially Sighted Children recommended that as far as possible these children should be educated in special classes in ordinary schools. The Board of Education Committee of Inquiry into the Problems Relating to Children with Defective Hearing reporting in 1938 recommended a three-fold classification: those whose hearing disabilities were such that they would benefit from an ordinary class with no special arrangements; those who required special arrangements and support in the ordinary school or a special school; and those who needed to be educated with the deaf.

The philosophy of the 1944 Education Act was clearly

influenced by the thinking of the Wood Committee and these other Committees. The Act was concerned with the provision of educational opportunities for all children and the establishment of a national framework which would aim to educate according to individual differences in age, aptitude and ability. The 'handicapped' were considered within the same legislative framework as normal children. The underlying principle of the 'normalization' of handicap was reflected in the wording of Section 33 (ii) which empowered local education authorities to provide special schools for children in the 'several categories of handicap', but (para. 2) 'where this is impracticable or where the disability is not serious, the arrangements may provide for the giving of such education in any school maintained or assisted by the local education authority'.

The Act created the term 'educational subnormality' as a replacement for 'educable mental defective'. It was intended to be descriptive rather than diagnostic and it changed the basis of the description for ascertainment purposes from intellectual deficiency to educational backwardness. The Handicapped Pupils and School Health Service Regulations of 1945 defined educationally subnormal pupils as 'pupils who by reason of limited ability or other conditions resulting in educational retardation require some form of education wholly or partly in substitution for education normally given in ordinary schools'.

Other categories defined by these regulations were the blind, partially sighted, deaf, partially hearing, epileptic, physically handicapped, speech defective, delicate and maladjusted. When maladjustment was included, it was the first time any statute had referred to this particular group as a separate category. Maladjusted children were those who were defined as psychologically disturbed or emotionally unstable and who required 'special educational treatment in order to effect their personal, social or educational readjustment'.

The diagnosis and treatment of handicapped children was the main point of intervention in the education system for educational psychologists. Although not officially named in Sections 33 and 34 in relation to ascertainment procedures, the educational psychologist had just claim to be the most likely person to develop services for the 'newer' handicaps of 'educational subnormality' and 'maladjustment'. Both handicaps could more easily be construed in educational/psychological than medical terms and it was educational psychology that provided the technology to enable concepts to be readily operationalized so that needs could be easily and 'objectively' identified. For the appraisal of ESN, despite the fact that the definition of this did not hinge on 'psychological' so much as 'educational' measures, the traditional individual intelligence test was usually the centre-piece of the diagnostic and assessment process. Once it had been decided that a child's attainments were such as to qualify him for special treatment the intelligence test was used as a device for ascertaining the form of special treatment that was required. 'Objective' psychological measures were no less important for the appraisal of maladjustment. Again IQ tests figured prominently even with children whose main handicap was thought to be behavioural or emotional rather than cognitive. Intelligence tests produced global measures but the quality of responses and the between sub-test variations in performance provided useful data on non-cognitive aspects of functioning. In practice, such tests tended to be used in preference to other seemingly more relevant techniques (e.g., projective tests) because they were considered to be more sound psychometrically.

It is no exaggeration to suggest that the development of special education was not only assisted by but in a sense made possible by the application of psychological techniques and findings. They served to legitimate diagnostic and assessment procedures and provided a rationale for the various definitions of handicap.

It is against this background of developments in special education that educational psychologists began to become established as an important professional grouping in local education authorities. We have so far discussed the contribution of the knowledge base. It now remains to take a closer look at the administrative and organizational base of the educational psychologist. But first, in order to avoid confusion, it will be necessary to look at the growth of an institution with which the educational psychologist has had and continues to have close links and with which he used to be closely identified.

THE CHILD GUIDANCE CLINIC

According to Sampson (1980) there were three important background features which influenced the development of child guidance clinics. The first was the Child Study Movement which made steady advances throughout the nineteenth century in Europe and America which resulted in the founding of the British Child Study Association in 1893. A feature of the Movement was that it brought together teachers, parents and specialists in a number of fields, and thus anticipated the concept of team-work — such an essential aspect of the principles on which child guidance clinics were founded. Intellectually the Movement reflected the new psychology and Sully, Burt and Winch all made substantial contributions, but, despite this, its general approach was rather amateurish and it increasingly came in for criticism from the purists. It undoubtedly played a major role in changing the climate of opinion on childhood and did much to publicize new ideas. It probably influenced the Board of Education Regulations for the Training of Teachers (1905) which in paragraph XXV stated that 'the teacher in training will gain much by watching some of the work that is now proceeding in the observation of children'.

The second influence came from the work of the early psychologists who pioneered approaches to the 'scientific' study of children. In 1884 Galton established his anthropological laboratory and this was followed in 1896 by Sully who opened a psychological laboratory in London to which teachers and parents were encouraged to bring their 'problem' children for assessment and treatment recommendations. Similar work was carried out by Burt in his laboratory at Liverpool which he began in 1907.

A third influence was the 'public concern' over delinquency and the link between delinquency and feeblemindedness. The moral depravity of the mentally handicapped was considered to be one of the main causes of delinquency. Just how concerned the public were is difficult to estimate, but certainly for the authorities the growing numbers of deliquents constituted a threat to the social order.

The history of child guidance clinics has been fraught with tensions of one kind or another which will be referred to again in more detail in the next chapter.

The first clinic was established in 1927 by the Jewish Health Organization and the second in 1928 under the auspices of the Child Guidance Council which was the British representative of the American Commonwealth Fund. Burt, who had already been working a child guidance system and psychological clinic of his own while in the employ of the London County Council, was approached to be the first director of the new clinic, but was unable to accept because of his other commitments and the team was led instead by Dr Moodie, a psychiatrist.

By 1932 there were six clinics in London financed by the fund and sited mostly in hospitals. They soon spread to the provinces and by 1935 eighteen clinics had been established. This year marked the end of the child guidance clinics movement's voluntary phase, and the beginning of full financial support from the local authorities. By the end of the Second World War there were approximately ninety-five such clinics.

Despite some local variations, the child guidance clinics

tended to be psychiatrically oriented and were usually under the direction of a psychiatrist. It is worth clarifying the distinction between a psychiatrist and a psychologist since doubt still remains in the public mind. The psychiatrist is medically qualified, although his medical background can vary from one with little training in child psychiatry to one with consultant status in this area. The educational psychologist has a degree in psychology or its equivalant, is usually a trained and experienced teacher and has a postgraduate professional qualification in educational psychology. Psychiatrists were the 'natural' leaders of the clinic teams (the core team consisted of psychiatrist, psychologist and social worker) partly because the rationale of the clinic was usually defined in mental health terms and partly because being members of a long-established and powerful profession their training was considered to be more substantial than either of the other two 'new' professions.

Of American origin, child guidance clinics represented an approach to the treatment of deliquency based on an understanding of the social and psychological pressures on the individual rather than on moral condemnation. As such they were part of the mental hygiene movement — a movement with origins in late nineteenth century philanthropy combined with a concern for control and direction of the 'dangerous classes'. It was a feature of the 'new humanism', as Platt (1969) describes it (a humanism which embraced the psychology as well as the psychiatry of the period) that crime was to be 'medicalized' and 'psychiatricized' and described and explained in terms which were allegedly morally neutral. This new definition was thus based on the 'medical model'. The psychiatry typically employed in child guidance clinics represented a new direction for that discipline, one increasingly influenced by psychoanalytic interpretations. This has led critics of psychoanalysis to link it with the more traditional aspects of the medical model.

The original focus of clinics was delinquency, but in Britain the range of problems with which they were concerned broadened to include many forms of disturbed and neurotic behaviour and general problems of mental health. After the 1944 Education Act they became the main institution for diagnosing children deemed to be maladjusted and for advising the local authority as to the most appropriate forms of treatment. Despite their origins and the medical influence, most clinics eventually fell under the auspices of the local education authorities to become part of a wider service concerned with the appraisal and guidance of children with special educational needs.

The strength of the child guidance clinic was allegedly in its concept of team-work. The rationale behind this was derived from the notion that the child should be looked at as a 'whole' or at least from as many different aspects as possible. The various disciplines of psychiatry, psychology and social work would make their own special contribution, and the information obtained from these three sources would be pooled to make up a complete picture of the child and his situation. The main instrument for facilitating this process was the case conference which involved all three core child guidance professions plus other relevant professionals such as psychotherapists, remedial teachers, ordinary class teachers or school medical officers.

Although a desirable idea in theory, the concept of the multidisciplinary team had its critics right from the beginning. In 1929, for example, the Psychiatry Section of the Royal Society of Medicine in the course of a debate on the 'Difficult Child' raised the problem of team-work with professions whose skills were difficult to estimate. There has always been the feeling among the medical profession that the confidentiality between patient and doctor might be violated in a team-work situation. The tensions arising from different professional perspectives on child guidance team-work will be discussed more fully in the next chapter.

THE SCHOOL PSYCHOLOGICAL SERVICE

Paralleling the educational psychologist's involvement in child guidance clinics was his work in the more educationally oriented school psychological service. The first official psychologists' office within an Education Department of a local authority was set up in 1913 by the London County Council and the first psychologist to be appointed was Cyril Burt. Burt's work covered the full range of activities that might be expected of a comprehensive school psychological service today, and established the guidelines for future developments. Like Binet, one of his major concerns was the examination of pupils in elementary schools who had been nominated for admission to special schools. A psychologist had been appointed for this task at the insistence of members of the London inspectorate who, among others, recommended the establishment of this new post rather than the appointment of an additional school medical officer, and it was to the inspectorate not the medical section that Burt was attached. A financial consideration was involved because it was felt that too many expensive mistakes had been made as a result of selecting children with pseudo-mental deficiency. This was blamed on the unreliable intellectual assessments carried out by doctors without benefit of psychological training.

But the diagnosis of mental deficiency was only one of Burt's many tasks. He was as much involved with applying psychology to the mainstream as the marginal areas of the education system. His 'Reports of the psychologist to the London Council' included references to the results of surveys of the abilities and attainments of the whole school population. He devoted a great deal of time to the construction of ability and educational tests and to the educational and vocational guidance of children within the 'normal' range as well as the seriously backward, disturbed and delinquent. One of his major concerns was to establish close co-operation with the schools which he saw as indispensable to good psychological practice, and he saw the psychologist as an education-based 'expert' under whose guidance the various special services could be integrated and related to the ongoing guidance function of ordinary schools.

The major expansion of the school psychological service did not take place until some time after the war for reasons that will be discussed later. Burt was the London Psychologist between 1913-32 before he transferred to University College, and he was not replaced until 1949. His career is interesting because he represented in one man the links that existed between psychological practice in schools, universities and local authorities — links which have been maintained ever since, and which were the foundation for all later developments.

It is worth noting that similar developments had been taking place in other parts of Europe. In France, Binet published a series of papers on individual psychology in 1896 and this was followed in 1904 by the first version of his intelligence test and in 1905 by the establishment of a pedagogical laboratory. He became a member of a Commission whose aim was to establish selection methods to differentiate between 'subnormals' and the 'mentally deficient'. It was proposed to the Minister of Public Instruction that a scheme be developed involving an examination of not only the medical but also the educational, psychological and social aspects of subnormality. In Germany, developments were more tentative. Stern established an Institute of Applied Psychology and was the first to suggest that the ratio of mental age to chronological age could be expressed as IQ. In Switzerland, the ideas and practices being developed by Claparède were probably more in line with the general directions of Burt's service. Despite initial opposition from various University faculties in Geneva, he in alliance with other pioneers established the *Institut des Sciences de l'Education* which made an important contribution to child study and experimental education. Links were established between training establishments, research and school services. Thus training courses for teachers, psychologists and social workers were developed alongside research programmes in educational psychology. These pioneering efforts were followed in 1920 by the setting up in Berne of *La Consultation Pédagogique*, and towards the end of the decade by a school psychological service with a wide range of functions.

Developments in America took a somewhat different turn. According to Wall (1956) American psychologists were perhaps overly influenced by the old associationist standpoint in its new behavioural clothing and were less concerned with studies of the all-round development of children which so much appealed to educators. Consequently, it was perhaps not surprising that in the early American clinics (on which British child guidance clinics were modelled) the role of the psychologist was conceived in narrow terms. Unfortunately, from the point of view of those advocating a broader role for the psychologist, it was the psychiatrists who had embraced and become more closely identified with the perspectives of the British psycho-biological school.

By the beginning of the war it could be said that although educational psychology as a subject had become established, the profession itself still had some way to go. Psychology and psychological techniques were clearly needed by the education system and were influencing policy and practice in a number of different areas. For educational psychologists, however, the inter-war years were something of an uncertain period. The child guidance clinic model was dominant during these years, which implied a narrower role for the psychologist than that envisaged on the basis of Burt's experience. In the next chapter, the emergence of the educational psychologist as a relatively more autonomous professional will be charted against the background of developments in the post-war reconstruction period.

CHAPTER 2

The emerging profession: post-war developments

The growing contribution of the EP can be set against a backcloth of developments in all aspects of welfare in the post-war reconstruction period. Taylor, Walton and Young (1975, page 10) refer to the concern of Fabian architects of welfare policies 'to win sections of the middle class to the struggle against those personal, social, environmental, educational and even spatial deprivations which helped to disqualify vast sections of the [working class] population from meaningful participation in the newly-reconstructing society'. This expanding army of personal service professionals or middle class 'helpers' or 'people professions' (see Ingleby, 1974) was involved with different institutions of the Welfare State but had in common a concern for 'deprivation' and 'opportunity'.

The EP was one among a number of these 'new' professions. His knowledge and skills were exactly what was required by the architects of social policy who had the problem of devising a system of distributing welfare resources on a socially just basis. If, in the words of George and Wilding (1976, page 132), 'The needs of the retarded child are greater than the needs of the normal child, just as those of the disabled are greater than those of the physically fit', then someone had to establish the criteria of need (when is a child retarded?) in a manner which could stand up to public scrutiny.Thus the need for the professional expert. Although there have always been criticisms of this approach, this has not prevented the increasing reliance on such expert opinion in the post-war years. Even modern critics of 'expertism' and advocates of what George and Wilding (page 135) describe as the 'populist' and 'comparative' approach rarely dismiss the professional contribution out of hand. It has been and is likely to remain an important prop of the welfare edifice.

Yet, like other 'new' professions educational psychologists have had to struggle for an identity in areas of practice which have traditionally been the preserve of older and more powerful professions like medicine. In recent years they have also been concerned with 'encroachment' by other emergent professions within education.

CHILD GUIDANCE

In the post-war period the EPs' professional struggles were nowhere more acute than in the child guidance clinic which was an inevitable tension point in the system. Even after the clarifications of Underwood (1955), it was still essentially an ambiguous and ill-defined area at the interface of medical, educational and social work institutions. The idea was ambitious — to deliver a service via a multidisciplinary team approach. The team was to consist of a psychiatrist, psychologist and psychiatric social worker who would each contribute their own special knowledge to the diagnosis and treatment recommendations which would therefore be based on a many-sided view of the child.

Uncertainties arose because it proved in practice extremely difficult to create a division of labour based on special contribution with which everyone agreed. In particular, there was a continuing tension between psychiatrist and psychologist over the scope of the psychologist's role in the set-up. Attempts to resolve this by formulating definitions giving equal weight to the value of both their contributions were usually so vague, imprecise and question-begging as to cloud the issue still further. For example, Davidson (1952) recalls how the difference between a psychologist and a psychiatrist was described by a psychiatrist in the following way:

> I (the psychiatrist) am saying to the patient 'I want to help you to get better developed and integrated' while you (the psychologist) are saying 'I want to find out about your abilities, attitudes and personality so that I can help you to find the means of using your good qualities effectively and of understanding yourself'.
> (page 3)

Role definitions were in fact negotiated in a context where power was not equally distributed among the members of the so-called team. As director of the clinic and as a member of an old and powerful profession the psychiatrist had a greater influence over 'reality definitions' than either the psychologist or the psychiatric social worker. For many educational psychologists this resulted in a diminution in their role to that of 'tester' and in many cases to tester of cognitive and not personality functions. Discussion of these issues was particularly vehement in the early 'fifties, although in some form or another the psychologist–psychiatrist relationship has always been and in may cases continues to be problematic. At that time, however, the relatively new and vigorous profession of educational psychology was emerging from the clouds which had overshadowed it in the interwar years.

The period was characterized by a flexing of muscles on both sides of the interface. An illustration of this is the argument that took place at the famous 'Symposium on psychologists and psychiatrists in the Child Guidance Service', reported in the *British Journal of Educational Psychology* between 1951 and 1953. In his conclusion, Burt (1953) referred to psychiatrists' over-concern with the 'pathological' which led them to see 'symptoms' in all children whereas in fact many of the 'difficult' or 'maladjusted' children referred were usually within the 'normal' range. He alleged that psychiatrists tended to treat maladjustment as a 'disability of mind' instead of regarding it as an interaction between personality and environment, and did not recognize that in 'thirty per cent of referrals some environmental handicap seems to be the main factor' (page 14). Psychiatrists tended to refer to 'maladjustment' or 'mental deficiency' as clear-cut clinical entities but the psychologist recognized that 'causal patterns varied from one individual to another' (page 21) and the same behaviour or condition could be linked with a variety of causes.

Other contributers to the symposium raised the issues of expense and effectiveness. Thus Banks (1953) considered that psychiatry's concern with the analysis of emotional problems in depth was not needed for most referrals. All that was required was 'a bit of re-education, sympathetic understanding and the inculcation of new habits and interests' (page 2). Banks, like Burt, also thought that psychological work was more effective because, unlike psychiatry which was mostly based on intelligent guesswork, it rested on 'a sound theoretical basis'. This author also provides an 'atrocity' story of what could happen if the physicalist, medical model were carried to its logical conclusion.

> To cure mental deficiency Sir Victor Hornley had introduced a surgical operation on the skull. He was reluctant to give figures for his results as are psychiatrists today; but later surgeons reported that the mortality was about 1 in 4 and those who survived revealed no improvement. (page 4)

References of this nature presented by psychologists to back their cases were clearly a sensationalist attempt to swing colleagues behind the banner. There was considerable feeling among psychologists at the time about what they regarded as the spurious knowledge base on which psychiatry rested. They particularly resented the claims made for the directorship of cases on the strength of a superior knowledge of 'depth' psychology. On the other hand, psychologists, psychiatrists claimed, had had success in removing symptoms and because of this 'they have become too ready to dispose of the interest of the psychiatrist in the deeper aspects of maladjustment as a morbid pre-occupation with psychopathology' (Moody 1952, page 158).

Feelings were running high in the build-up to the publication of the Underwood Report (1955) which, it was hoped, would provide a rational framework within which it would be possible for professionals from different disciplines to work together in a well-organized and comprehensive Child Guidance Service. However, like the Summerfield Report thirteen years later, Underwood went so far, but, certainly as far as the more militant educational psychologists were concerned, did not go far enough. Underwood implied, as Williams (1974) points out that

> ... educational psychologists would only spend half of their time in the clinic. For the other half of their time they would work from the education department, operating a service for the schools (now semi-officially called a School Psychological Service) which would deal with a wider variety of problems than those *seriously deviant* children who were referred to the Child Guidance Clinic. (page 6)

Such an arrangement smacked of a two-tier system. Acting on the basis outlined as a referral agency to the CGC, the SPS might be considered as dealing with 'less serious' cases with the implication that CGC was a more high-powered set-up. While the clinic hierarchy was retained the educational psychologist would almost certainly not be able to determine his own role with the degree of autonomy he would have liked. Moreover, for many educational psychologists, it would have meant spending a considerable proportion of their valuable time working within a system with whose basic diagnostic and treatment philosophy they profoundly disagreed.

THE SCHOOL PSYCHOLOGICAL SERVICE

It is interesting to compare the Underwood view of the School Psychological Services as a 'footnote' to the Child Guidance Clinic with the view expressed in a UNESCO document published one year later in 1956. Drawing on European experience, Wall and his co-workers provided a description of the functions of the School Psychological Service which in many respects was more radical and more like the modern conception than that contained in the Summerfield Report some twelve years later.

They saw the School Psychological Service as part and parcel of the general trend of applying psychology to schools, and therefore part of a process that was concerned with a broad range of educational and psychological issues. Basically the contemporary school had three tasks which were particularly amenable to psychological help and advice. These involved activities relating to the problem of guidance, the problem of adaptation of methods and curricula and the discovery and remediation of exceptional children. Guidance was a particularly important part of the teacher's role but, it was alleged, could not be discharged unaided by the teacher. The problem was particularly relevant to secondary level where various choices had to be made at certain crucial points in the child's educational career. Curricula and method needed to take into account the basic 'rhythms of child development' and the more research produced knowledge about the latter the more psychological advice was relevant to changing the former. In relation to exceptional children, teachers needed to be sensitized to the early signs of difficulty, as well as to the needs of those whose difficulties were full blown. Wall *et al* saw the School Psychological Service as deeply involved in all these tasks in close collaboration with teachers and other specialist services.

Specifically the function of the school or educational psychologist was to collaborate with teachers in relation to the educational guidance of all pupils; to be especially concerned with the maintenance of up to date, relevant information on the record cards for each pupil; to work to improve educational methods and the social climate of the classroom; to co-operate with teachers and in many cases assume major responsibility for liaison between different services. As far as possible, links with the school should be such that the school psychologists should regularly take part in staff meetings.

In general terms, the service should contain under its umbrella the specialized units of child guidance, remedial teaching, speech re-education and be closely associated with special schools or classes and with institutions concerned with vocational guidance. It should co-operate with the school medical service but not be subordinate to it, and should be more concerned with prevention than treatment. It should have close links with university research and training departments, and should participate in research projects. The educational psychologist was considered to be the most appropriate professional to direct and adminster this service. It was felt that because of his background in teaching and psychology he could act as a bridge between the schools and the various services more easily than any other professional. He was also the only person whose psychological knowledge was likely to be complete and up to date.

For an EP who supported the UNESCO model, the situation regarding his role in the British education system was clearly not satisfactory. The institutional frameworks established in the interwar years were still alive and well and not working in his favour.

THE ASSOCIATION OF EDUCATIONAL PSYCHOLOGISTS

Such discontents among educational psychologists, their renewed confidence as LEAs began to show more interest in implementing the 1944 Act in the SE (Special Education) area and certain differences of interest between themselves and their academic colleagues in the British Psychological Society were among the factors contributing to the setting up of the Association of Educational Psychologists in 1962. The nature of this new body was described by Roe, a leading member of the executive and editor of the *Newsletter*, in an editorial entitled 'Creating a viable ambiance' (Sept. 1964). He wrote:

> It is generally accepted, we think, that a Trade Union exists not only to guard the interests of its members in wage and salary negotiations with their employers but also to maintain standards of skill and professional pride in the mystery of their craft. There is a continuum between the BMA and the T&GWU.

Like other professional associations in education it endeavoured to maintain an image of an organization as much devoted to the development of education services catering for the needs of children and young people as to the furtherance of its own salary, status and 'territorial' interests. It was from the start an organization that believed in vigourously maintaining the base in education and has always insisted that educational psychologists as well as having qualifications at degree level in psychology and postgraduate training in educational psychology should also be experienced and qualified teachers. This was very much a case of an organization playing to its strength in its attempts to maintain and improve the professional status of its members. Educational psychologists had a long history of working within an educational framework and it was education that provided the major source of support in their various struggles. For example, in the struggle over child guidance they were powerfully backed by a number of important educational organizations. Sir William Alexander, Chairman of the Association of Education Committees, had reported (1964) that this body had been advocating since 1946 that the Child Guidance Service should be an integral part of the Education Service. In his view there was 'no possible doubt that the key person in the Child Guidance Service is the educational psychologist...' He thought it highly desirable that an educational psychologist should also be a teacher.

Clearly, whatever other reason the AEP might have had for retaining the teaching component as an essential part of their qualifications, an enhanced and more secure professional status under the education umbrella was probably the most significant. And within education, of course, they were more than just equivalent to an ordinary teacher. Their experience and extra training meant that their relationship to teachers was, as Alexander put it, like 'consultant to general practitioner'.

Yet the base in education, supportive as it was, by no means dispersed all uncertainties. As the profession grew in the 'sixties and became increasingly entrenched as part of the educational establishment, the optimism exuded prior to the publication of the Summerfield Report (1968) was always edged with a certain nervousness. Thus, despite support from the AEC, and despite the 'end of an era of isolation and uncertainty', Bannon (1965) reporting from the Presidential Chair of the AEP still saw the necessity for EPs 'to continue to strive for recognition and status in the education world'. And Reid in the same year, while being initially optimistic that 'when professional disciplines fully know their own roles, then it is possible for there to be genuine team work' (page 3) goes on to conclude ominously that in his view psychiatrists' training as doctors 'predisposes them to see their profession as the only discipline that can hold all the responsibility for health, mental and physical' (page 4).

Nevertheless, in their more buoyant moments, their embrace was perceived as expansive. Child guidance, broadly interpreted, was the whole of education, and part of the role of the educational psychologist was to keep 'the door of opportunity' open to all children, 'the slow and the quick to pursue their bent according to their age, aptitude and ability' (James 1964). The prospects for 'consultant' status within education were good.

THE SUMMERFIELD REPORT

For those who were looking forward to official recognition of the broader role of EPs, the Summerfield Report (1968) was something of a disappointment. It was largely a reflection of existing practice rather than a model for the future. For example, according to one commentator in the AEP *Journal and Newsletter* (1968), the report assumed that educational psychologists were always concerned mainly with 'Wednesday's child and not, for example, the aims of education and curricular developments generally for which the educational psychologist by dint of training and experience could make a useful contribution' (G. Robb, page 32). Moreover, as another prominent commentator pointed out in the same issue (page 25), the report was not critical enough of the weaknesses of the present system. It failed 'to comment on the weaknesses of the present CGC organisation and practice' and was not sensitive to the fact that 'there are still areas where educational psychologists experience difficulty in acting in their rightful role as educational specialists because psychiatrists claim the right to decide on all forms of treatment including educational'.

There were complaints of a tendency in Summerfield to be overly influenced by the Underwood model, and thus to lay too great an amphasis on the CGC role and not to recognize the rapidly expanding role of the educational psychologist in education as a whole.

Another area of concern was the role of the School Health Service in the ascertainment of children requiring special educational treatment because of educational subnormality. It should be remembered that there had been no mention of educational psychology in relation to these procedures in the 1944 Act, despite the fact that, as has been suggested, the spirit of the Act accorded with the psycho-educational model of 'handicap'. Section 34 (1) of the Act stated that:

> It shall be the duty of every local education authority to ascertain what children in their area require special educational treatment, and for the purpose of fulfilling that duty any officer . . . may by notice in writing served upon the parent of any child who has attained the age of two years require him to submit for examination by a medical officer of the authority for advice as to whether

the child is suffering from any disability of mind or body and as to its nature or extent of any such disability . . .

In performing this function school medical officers normally carried out psychological as well as medical assessments on which to base their advice to the authority. It was not mandatory for local education authorities to employ psychologists for these purposes, even though in many areas educational psychologists were an integral part of the procedure. However, although it is true that with respect to formal ascertainment the MOH or the Chief Education Officer did often request the EP to fill in the appropriate section of the 2HP form, there was no doubt that in many authorities SMOs were continuing to adminster psychological tests, e.g., the Stanford Binet, and to be ones whose advice was more regularly sought. Summerfield's view on this was that the question was not one of 'advisability' so much as 'practicability'. There were so many ESN children that 'It would clearly be unrealistic to expect educational psychologists to undertake the whole of this work at present, when they have many other commitments and their numbers are small' (Appendix 6A, page 157).

But perhaps one of the most significant features of the commets on Summerfield as reported in the *Journal and Newsletter* was the split that was revealed regarding the recommendation that, because of the need to increase supply rapidly, a Route 3 training procedure should be allowed whereby honours graduates in psychology could become EPs without having qualified as teachers or having had teaching experience in schools. A number of educational psychologists felt that although teaching experience was desirable it should not be essential to train as a teacher before training to be a psychologist. For example, Crabtree (1968, page 24) considered that educational psychologists were psychologists first and teachers second; they were not received as 'better teachers than teachers, and should not set themselves up as such; that when asked to give an opinion on a child, for example, it was their psychological background and clinic training that they drew upon rather than teaching experience'.

Such arguments were vigorously opposed by other contributers to the discussion. As we have seen, the teaching component was an important part of the AEP strategy for improving the status of educational psychologists under education and thus enabling them to receive increased backing from education in their relations with other professionals. Those who opposed the teaching component (i.e., opposed the idea that the teacher qualification was essential) were mainly concerned with the niceties of the debate such as whether other kinds of experience with children were just as valuable as teaching experience in schools. The debate, however, was not really about the value of teaching experience so much as whether or not a major plank of AEP policy should be preserved.

In the event, as subsequent statements of the executive showed, the AEP policy on this matter held firm. What was revealed by this discussion, however, were the splits in the ranks between those who were for and those who were against this particular aspect of policy. Thus, in addition to various external pressures and constraints, educational psychologists had to contend with those which emanated from their own colleagues. Those who opposed the teaching component were, in fact, a minority, but their presence did mean that the AEP's negotiating position was somewhat weakened because the profession was seen to lack unity.

The question of unity has always been relevant to negotiations with the DES, particularly over the questions of registration and mandatory School Psychological Services, neither of which were guaranteed by Summerfield.

However, if Summerfield was not to the liking of all EPs it at least had the positive function of reinforcing this status quo. Even if it did recommend 'more of the same', it wanted a lot more of it — an increased output of EPs from training establishments involving an input to education of three times the then current number by 1975 and the planning of services on the assumption that one EP was required for every 10,000 schoolchildren. There was an emphasis on expansion; educational psychology was and continued to remain in a growth phase. The numbers rose from 320 in 1965 to 440 in 1967 to approximately 460 at the time of Summerfield and accelerated to 500 by 1970 and 640 by 1972 (see Williams, P. 1974 page 8).

THE 'COMING OF AGE'

The mid 'seventies, though a period of retrenchment and taking stock for education as a whole, may be looked upon as a period when School Psychological Services finally 'came of age' (see Wright, 1975). Circular 2/75 suggested procedures for the discovery, diagnosis and assessment of children with special needs which indicated that recommendations for special educational treatment should not be made by a medical officer but by an educationalist — in most cases an educational psychologist. The new forms to replace the old HP (Handicapped Pupils) Forms 1–5 were to be called SE (Special Education) Forms 1-6. These were welcomed by EPs because of the change of emphasis from 'handicap' to special educational needs and because the EP would be given more direct responsibility for assessment (see AEP, 1975). In general, there was support for 2/75 on the grounds that it emphasized educational criteria and abolished medical or quasi-medical terminology, e.g., 'ascertainment' (see AEP, 1977).

Another important circular, 3/74, issued by the DES, DHSS and the Welsh Office, advocated a network of Child Guidance Services, including School Psychological Services, which would collaborate with each other in different combinations according to need but which would each be independent organizations with their own premises.

The official recognition of EPs in these circulars certainly represented a step forward for the profession, but it would be easy to exaggerate the advances in security and status that they provided. Other changes took place in the mid 'seventies which could easily be underestimated in terms of their implications for the status and role of EPs. Ravenette, the AEP President, considered that the administrative changes in local authority and health services were even more significant for EPs than the Summerfield Report. That Report essentially rationalized existing structures and trends, whereas the new arrangements of the mid 'seventies created new bureaucratic entities with which EPs were forced to come to terms. In Ravenette's view (1974) EPs in fact lost out in the scramble for position in the 'new hierarchies' to inspectors and advisors, and struggles developed within education departments for the 'ownership' of School Psychological Services. There was something of a crisis here for EPs who, as we have seen, relied on education for support. New professions, e.g., advisers, were growing up under the umbrella of education with as much right to make decisions about certain aspects of special education procedures as EPs. Ground was being cut from the EPs' feet not from without but from within their chosen haven.

However, for Ravenette, developments in the health service were 'potentially far more threatening'. Clinical psychologists were re-examining their role and there was the possibility of encroachment on the traditional territory of the EP. The idea of a new profession of 'child psychologist', for long the cherished hope of academic psychologists, was being seriously proposed.

The AEP was quick to state its views on both these issues. At an informal meeting with the DES the representatives expressed concern at 'the inevitable limitations of "child psychologists" without an adequate teaching background' (see AEP 1976). In the debate on this question the teaching component was again argued for strongly by the AEP. In their representation to the DES the value of the teaching component was reaffirmed and the reasons were spelt out clearly. First, as EPs' work contained a substantial advisory element, personal knowledge of the school context was essential. Second, there was the recent precedent of the Arbitration Panel, when considering salaries, having accepted the 'affinity to teaching' argument and third, the 'bridge' function between the various services — health, education and social services — was facilitated by the particular training and experience of the EP. In general, it was felt by the AEP that special educational resources should be used efficiently, particularly in a period of cutbacks and that the creation of a new and therefore untried and questionable additional profession dealing with children was not really what was required.

There were also important conceptual differences between academics and practising EPs, as represented by the AEP, on this subject. Ravenette (1974), for example, considered that the 'essence of the task [i.e. the practice of educational psychology] is not the work with the child but the ability to operate within the different contexts which provided the original problem whereby the child was in fact interviewed' (page 3). The label of child psychologist gave a 'false description' and 'blurred the distinction' between clinical and educational psychologists.

In a very real sense discussion of the child psychology proposal can be seen as the latest round in the ever-continuing conflict between one group of psychologists and another over the teaching component. In June 1976 the AEP sent a forceful reminder about their position to Professor Hetherington, Secretary General of the BPS, in connection with the Working Party on Child Psychologists set up under the BPS auspices. Such a profession would be deficient in skills needed by local authorities, e.g., advisory skills in schools, skills in assessing special educational needs, and even clinical skills. This missive also suggested what was perhaps the AEP's view of the real motive behind the proposal: 'The suggestion for this variation of applied psychologist will no doubt provide an outlet for redundant research workers or for undergraduates who see a possible short cut to psychological work with children'.

THE COURT AND TRETHOWAN REPORTS

One consequence of the local government reorganization referred to above was that a new look at the organization of child health services was considered necessary. The Court Committee was set up to report on this very matter and it published its recommendations in 1976. It was also necessary to consider the role of clinical psychologists in the newly reorganized health service and this was the subject of the Trethowan Report. In each report there was considerable discussion about the organization of psychological services for children.

As far as EPs were concerned, one of the significant features here was that in certain crucial respects the reports contradicted each other. Trethowan suggested that the best way to achieve an integrated child psychology service was via co-operation between individual psychologists, while paragraph 14.35 of the Court Report recommended the creation of an integrated child psychology service, to be considered in relation to whether it should be independently organized or under health, education or social services.

The AEP had already been indicating that it would support an independent psychology service for children and young people provided this was based within education departments of local authorities, and was also on record as considering it to be a wasteful overlap if specialities were developed for psychological work with children in both the National Health and Education Services (see comments on Trethowan). Thus not only did the reports contradict each other, but they failed to respond to the AEP's arguments for an independent child psychology service, which were well known prior to the publication of both reports. They also failed to appreciate the wide-ranging nature of EPs' skills in the treatment as well as diagnostic areas.

The second contradiction between the Reports was over the question of clinical psychologists' 'right to entry' to schools. In paragraph 14.36 of Court it was recommended that in view of their expanded role and community orientation clinical psychologists should have an automatic right of access to schools whereas Trethowan indicated that EPs should have the power to veto the entry rights to school of their clinical colleagues. Clearly, the forces opposing the AEP line on these issues were in disarray.

An intriguing aspect of all this was the way in which the AEP was provided with information about the Trethowan Report. The Court Report showed that Trethowan had been compiled in 1974 but since 1973, when the AEP was asked to give evidence, no further information had been forthcoming. Eventually after repeated requests to the Secretary of State for Health and Social Security and after 'acknowledged support' from the NUT, the Society of Education Officers, Association of Education Committees and MPs who asked questions in the House of Commons, the AEP was sent a copy of the Report (see AEP, 1977). Would the AEP have been justified in thinking foul play was afoot?

The reaction of many EPs to the Court Report was favourable in so far as the report was concerned with a serious attempt to rationalize health services for children, but there was alarm at the way Court's recommendations relating specifically to psychologists were based on premises about the role of EPs which, in the words of one commentator, were 'pure mythology' (see Love, 1977).

It was assumed, for example, (see paragraph 14.33) that clinical psychologists had more to do with young handicapped children, more skills and experience in relation to work with families and more involvement with the treatment of children with psychiatric disorders. In fact, in the view of EPs nothing could be further from the truth. There was empirical evidence to show that EPs were just as likely to be involved in these areas as clinicals. They spent much more of their time than clinicals in activities where the child was the main client (Love, 1977, page 4). As for treatment, a casual glance at the AEP *Journal and Newsletter* would have been enough to convince anyone that EPs were heavily involved here too — for example, the current spate of articles on behaviour modification programmes. As the AEP pointed out in its commentary on *Fit for the Future* (see AEP, 1977) 'more than half the referrals [i.e., to EPs] presented as behavioural and emotional problems'. Court failed to recognize that under the heading of 'advice' or 'consultation' was a great deal which in fact involved prescription of treatment. EPs had a broad role in education departments which meant that they acted as consultants to teachers who carried out the treatment programmes under their overall supervision.

Underlying the attitude of the AEP to Court's delineation of function between clinicals and educationals was possibly the fear that extending the influence of the former was tantamount to the reassertion of medical dominance. Although clinicals were striving to move out of hospitals into the 'community', most of them were still hospital based and, as Love (1977) has indicated, ninety-five per cent of their referrals were from psychiatrists. The Trethowan Report attempted to resolve the problems of clinical psychologists' autonomy under the NHS by proposing the time-worn strategy of decision making under the auspices of a multi-disciplinary team. EPs have had a long and rather bitter experience of this strategy; often the medically-directed CGC was a team in name only. There was thus a natural suspicion of any proposal for a team which involved the participation of medical personnel.

A close reading of Trethowan suggests that there may have been good grounds for these fears. For instance, the clinicals' dilemma is not altogether resolved by the following paragraph (52.5):

> ... if a need is identified for a particular procedure or programme which the psychologist is best equipped to apply, it seems to us right that he should be recognised as carrying responsibility, within such limits as may be agreed with other members of the team, for that aspect of the patient's treatment and care. There should be no question, therefore, of the patient's medical interests being jeopardised.

Prior to this a distinction is drawn between 'independent professional status' and 'full clinical responsibility which in the National Health Service can be excercised only by certain medical practitioners'. Although this appears to provide a framework for decision making which is democratic, in fact it is difficult to see how within the accepted definition of professional autonomy it is possible to arrive at an arrangement whereby one professional member would allow the other members of a team from different professions to decide what was within his competence. Moreover, it is based on the assumption that there are reasonably clear boundaries between the disciplines and that these boundaries are acceptable to the constituents, which, as the experience of EPs shows, is not necessarily correct. Even assuming that this ideal democratic set-up worked smoothly, it is not clear whether or not the medical practitioner involved would be required to accept any limitations the team might wish to place on his competence. Paragraph 5:2.3 includes the following sentence: 'We fully recognise that for any patient under treatment in the National Health Service, there is a continuing medical responsibility which cannot be handed over to any other profession'.

In view of these doubts and ambiguities it was not surprising perhaps that the AEP should be concerned about 'encroachment' by clinicals. At the AGM in 1978 among resolutions calling for action by the EC was one that supported the Association's policy on the non-supervision of clinical psychologists on field placement and another on the recommendation that all psychological work with children should be carried out by qualified EPs.

In one form or another, then, the 'medical threat' has been a major preoccupation of the AEP leadership and many rank and file EPs since the early days of the profession. The editor of the AEP *Journal and Newsletter* provides a vivid summing up of the position to date (Reid, R. S., 1978, page 47-8). 'In my lifetime

The emerging profession: post-war developments / 35

we educational psychologists are as a profession slowly advancing from the colonial status in which we were held by the medical profession', but despite circulars 3/74 and 2/75 'victory and independence have not been won. Old attitudes take an unconscionable time a-dying'.

He goes on to warn EPs that they should be prepared for counter attacks from psychiatrists and the old school medical officers via such institutions as District Handicap Teams recommended by the Court Report.

Other commentators have also noted the dangers of increased medical influence through the new and apparently democratic institutions proposed in recent reports. Where, asks Love (1977) would District Handicap Teams be based — in District General Hospitals? The AEP in its comments on Court opposed the idea of district networks needing hospital-based classrooms, arguing that it would obviously help integration if they were school based.

Court's conceptualization of the DHT contained assumptions about EPs' work which were unacceptable to the AEP since they were based on a restricted view of their role. The report also made recommendations about the subsumption of child guidance under child psychiatric services which were against the spirit of Circular 3/74. This had suggested that child guidance should be multi-service based and involve collaborative multidisciplinary network arrangements.

THE WARNOCK REPORT

Finally, mention should be made of the recommendations of Warnock (1979) relating to the role of the EP in special education. The Committee recognized three kinds of contributions from EPs in relation to the discovery of and assessment of special needs: (a) their specialized knowledge of observation techniques and assessment procedures which would help teachers with school-based assessment; (b) involvement with assessment of children with SEN at a more advanced stage of the assessment process; and (c) involvement with the 'monitoring of whole age groups of children at different stages during their school life' (para. 14.7).

In many ways, Warnock contained much that appealed to EPs, particularly in relation to the 'threats' to the profession discussed in this chapter, because it clarified the boundaries of medical intervention and recognized the contribution of the EP in areas where there had been ambiguity in the past. It criticized the

Court Report for using the term 'children with psychiatric disorders' and considered this to be less satisfactory than terms like 'children with emotional and behavioural disorders' or 'maladjusted children' (para. 14.8). It recognized the central role of the EP in dealing with these problems in school: 'In our view psychologists, working where necessary with psychiatrists and social workers, should remain foremost in helping teachers to deal with emotional and behavioural problems when they occur in school' (p. 148). And on the question of the location of District Handicap Teams it had this to say:

> Any team which is hospital-based is likely to develop a predominantly medically orientated approach. While this may be necessary for some children, particularly those with severe or complex disorders who require a period of specialist observation and testing, it is less likely to be suitable for those who, though they need special education provision, do not require hospital treatment. We therefore recommend that multi-professional assessment at Stage 5 should usually take place at a centre within the community other than a hospital. (para. 4.55)

However, although most of the Report was acceptable to EPs, there were still some proposals which if implemented were likely to diminish rather than extend their established role. Consequently the profession was still perceived as being under 'threat', the only difference being that this was seen as coming from a different direction. The AEP provided intimations of this in its comments on the Consultative Document (1978). It rejected Paragraph 4.62 which proposed that responsibility for SE procedures should be delegated to the proposed Special Education Advisory and Support Services. This would provide additional unnecessary 'link-personnel' between EPs and teacher colleagues. It considered that this proposal reflected the Warnock Committee's lack of appreciation of the functions of local authority psychological services.

> The Committee gives the impression of failing to comprehend the way in which the 'treatment' function of psychologists working in education services has evolved. The educational psychologist's keen understanding of the essentially educational/developmental nature of the strategies required for help has led to an essentially advisory role ... it is not always appropriate for such advice in relation to schools to be seen as geared solely to an individual pupil.

By ignoring this, the AEP felt that the Committee had created a situation which could lead to 'role conflict'.

THE ADVISORY SERVICE

In view of the AEP's reaction to Warnock, it might be appropriate to conclude this section with a brief word about the role of local authority advisers and their relationship to EPs. Among the first remedial teachers were those who had close connections with child guidance and school psychological services. Indeed, it was psychologists in the shape of F. J. Schonell and W. D. Wall who established the notion of a remedial education specialist in the first instance. Their Remedial Education Centre which opened in 1948 provided a practical basis for one-year courses for teachers specializing in remedial education. From these beginnings the remedial teaching profession grew and provided the reservoir of talent from which remedial advisers were drawn. Psychologists were also involved in the creation of training courses for special education, and continue to provide teachers in special education with in-service training.

EPs are always claiming that their aim is to do themselves out of a job and in the case of remedial education they have succeeded, up to a point. They have rarely wanted to be administratively responsible for running remedial services, but the responsibilities which have accrued over the years to remedial specialists and advisers have meant that EPs have to some extent been pushed into the background as the first source of support for the class teacher. Decisions are made about children with learning difficulties which result in children being selected (or not selected) for psychological referral on the basis of evidence which an EP in his expert wisdom might wish to question, if he had the choice to do so.

The role of the adviser in remedial or special education is, in effect, similar to the role the EP used to play and still does play in many areas. But for the EP there is one crucial difference. In its comments on the aforementioned Court Report, which also refers to advisers, the AEP noted that the Report failed to recognize the 'breadth' of the EPs contribution, 'instead it would be interpreted as suggesting that a psychologist *and* a *teacher and* an LEA adviser could do the work of a single EP'. It felt that advisers lacked training in 'scientific investigation' of individual problems and were without 'case study' background. Thus it was not only medics who posed a 'threat' to the profession. Here, the boundaries between adviser and psychologist were clearly drawn.

THE EDUCATIONAL PSYCHOLOGIST TODAY

In this chapter an attempt has been made to illuminate the development of the profession in the post-war period by focusing on certain crucial tension points the resolution of which was essential for professional survival. By and large, one would agree that by the end of the 'seventies educational psychologists had established themselves as a recognized professional grouping within education and that Wright's description of them having 'come of age' was essentially correct.

Educational psychologists today usually have a much broader role than they did in the pre-war and post-war periods. According to the enquiry carried out by the Division of Education and Child Psychology (1978), EPs are involved with a wide variety of problems; spend more time in schools than in any other setting and have more contact with teachers than they do with any other profession; and for a significant percentage of their time they are involved in policy, advisory and indirect treatment matters. They continue to work in multidisciplinary teams, but as Wright and Payne (1979) in their analysis of one service, point out, the composition of these teams usually varies according to need and the child guidance clinic team is only one among several with which EPs may become involved. In many respects, developments have followed the path suggested by Wall (1956). EPs collaborate with a variety of professions — clinical medical officers, teachers, social workers, speech therapists, etc. — in making their contribution to a network of services designed to cater for children's education, health and welfare needs. The historic link with the child guidance clinic is still maintained in most areas, but its importance has been reduced as other services, particularly the school psychological service, have developed. In the current situation, the 'togetherness' of the traditional team is threatened by the fact that the three core members are now employees of three distinct bodies: the psychiatrist is employed by the Regional Health Authority, the educational psychologist by the Local Education Authority and the social worker by the Local Authority Social Services Department. A typical arrangement is for clinics to be education rather than hospital based as part of a child guidance and school psychological service with the principal education psychologist in charge of overall services but with individual clinics working under the professional responsibility of a psychiatrist.

Yet it is still the case that many educational psychologists are having to work in situations where their role is distinctly limited in scope. They are still spending more time on assessment and placement work than on any other activity, which, according to the DECP study, 'does not represent the apportioning of time which EPs would like' (p. 12). In fact, the current situation constitutes something of a dilemma for EPs. On the one hand they would like to spend more time on advisory and treatment activities, but on the other their 'coming of age' relies on their having achieved official recognition for their contribution to assessment procedures as required in Circular 2/75.

Even if they wanted to, it would be difficult for EPs to ignore the importance of this official recognition. It is the foundation stone on which other aspects of the service are based and which, more importantly from a 'survival' viewpoint, provides EPs with a niche in local authorities which could not easily be filled by any other profession. It provides security for a profession which continues to feel that the problem of maintaining its identity and retaining status *vis-à-vis* other groupings is one that it ignores at its peril. As indicated above, as late as 1978, in the view of certain leading members of the profession, the 'medical threat' was still of some concern. The 'threat' from advisers and other educational specialists is perhaps even more significant.

A consequence of this preoccupation with boundary maintaining activities is that many EPs, though they aspire to be innovative, feel the necessity to cling to what they regard as their 'special contribution' to education. In practice this means working with a particularly narrow view of psychology in the context of the 'special' area of the education system.

CHAPTER 3

Psychometrics, professional survival and the traditional practitioner paradigm

Psychometrics in the form of intelligence testing has often been regarded as the 'cornerstone' of the EP's expertise. It was this aspect of the knowledge base that enabled him to make a special contribution to the selection of children for special education and was the most visible example of the 'scientific' knowledge base on which his identity was founded. Small wonder, then, that when, in the 'fifties, psychometrics came under attack from politicians, academics, teachers and others involved in the comprehensive school movement, the profession should feel the need to review its position in relation to the concept of intelligence and intelligence testing. This was carried out throughout the 'sixties and by the end of that decade, by the time Summerfield had reported, a rough consensus had been achieved among many of the leading lights in the profession. By the early 'seventies intelligence testing was again fairly entrenched as a vital part of the EPs' special knowledge. Presland (1970) comments that 'Except for intelligence testing... there is little objective evidence to help us differentiate between those children who need to go to ESN school and those who should stay in the ordinary school' (p. 14). Despite the general recognition of the socially constructed nature of intelligence test scores, for this leading psychologist as for many others, they represented the one solid 'fact' amid an array of speculative comment. However, the 'seventies as a whole were not chracterized by this kind of certainty about the value of psychometrics. In addition to unassuaged critics from outside the profession, practitioners themselves began to voice their own misgivings.

PRACTITIONER CRITICISMS

In recent years even some of the more conventional practitioners have sought to move away from the assessment and disposal role for which psychometric 'tools' were ideally suited, towards a role that involved developing strategies more directly useful to the class teacher. There has been an increasing emphasis on developing remedial programmes and curricula based on a detailed account of instructional objectives, and involving a different approach to diagnostic work. In pursuit of these objectives, time spent giving an individual intelligence test was at best of marginal use and at worst time totally wasted. Rather than spending up to an hour carefully administering a test the main aim of which was to find out the child's intellectual status in relation to his peers, far better to use the time more productively in finding out what the child could and could not do in relation to the curriculum of the school he attended and what modifications to that curriculum and/or teaching methods were required to help him make progress. Ideally, perhaps, there should be enough time for both these activities and more, but for hard-pressed practitioners it was a question of priorities, and for many EPs the old routine of administering the intelligence test as first priority was questioned.

The main thrust of this new emphasis was that it involved the EP in making a much closer contact with the school than he might have had previously. It was not enough to chat to the teacher and the headteacher and then write a report consisting mainly of the results of intelligence tests with interpretation. Now, in order to make a sensible diagnosis, the EP had to have far more detailed knowledge of the curriculum as it was actually being operated in the classroom, and this entailed more classroom observation, more communication with the class teacher and probably, in the period of remediation, more frequent visits to the school in an advisory role.

As noted in previous chapters, there was nothing particularly new in this emphasis, but for various reasons EPs had found it difficult to escape from being over-identified with psychometrics. In part they had only themselves to blame for this. Despite the growing criticism, too many EPs had accepted the psychometrically-oriented role.

THE PREOCCUPATION WITH TESTING

Not only does an overemphasis on psychometrics have implications for the practical activities of EPs, but it also influences their perspective on the theoretical resources which are perceived as being at their disposal. In theory, the EPs should be a reservoir of psychological knowledge which the educator can draw upon in relation to just about any problem. Unfortunately, there is evidence to suggest that many EPs do not quite see it in this way, and have maintained a view of their knowledge which places psychometrics at the core. Responses to a questionnaire sent out by Phillips (1974) to former trainees suggested an overwhelming emphasis on the importance of individual psychological assessment in practical work and the administration/evaluation of psychological tests/assessment techniques.

Much of the conventional literature also reinforces this preoccupation with psychometrics. In Chazan *et al* (1974), to date the only British text book in the practice of educational psychology, the chapter on 'theoretical' matters is solely concerned with the construction, standardization, validity, reliability and interpretation of educational and psychological tests. There are also chapters on assessment procedures in schools and techniques of individual assessment, but no chapter directly concerned with the broad range of theoretical knowledge which might be at the disposal of the EP. In a defence of the profession, Cooke (1977) describes the core skills of the EP as: (a) the application of scientific method; (b) psychometrics; (c) training and practical experience; and (d) liaison and entrepreneurial skills. Thus the only specific content mentioned, i.e., psychometrics, is that which provides a theoretical underpinning for assessment procedures.

Psychometrics have been dominant, then, partly because EPs themselves have tended to treat them as the 'core' of their professional knowledge. Another reason and one which clearly interacts with this is the tendency for other professionals and lay persons to focus on 'intelligence and intelligence testing' as a key aspect of the EP's identity — an identity institutionalized by the role in special education procedures. Even in areas where the other professionals appreciate that the EP has a broader role there is still a tendency for them to perceive this role differently from the EPs themselves, usually in terms which, from the EPs' viewpoint, exaggerate the importance of psychometric assessments. This contention is supported by some research carried out in one local authority by Freeman and Topping (1976) where it was found that different professional groups (headteachers, administrators, social workers, clinical medical officers and psychiatrists) had different expectations of EPs, and none of these groups had expectations which were the same as the EPs had of themselves.

Some EPs feel that there is no good reason why such

importance should be attached to the theory and practice of psychometrics. Although individual intelligence tests play a useful part in diagnosis and assessment for special education, they are not appropriate tools to use in all cases, as a matter of routine. EPs perceive themselves as psychologists not psychometricians, as consultants rather than technicians. An intelligence test is a 'tool' and its use is determined not by an administrative decision but by the professional decision of a consultant, who has a variety of options open to him as to how he wishes to use the test, in what form he wishes to present the results and how he wishes to interpret the results. Because it is a tool rather than the job itself, there is no reason why it should always be such a dominant feature of psychological practice. Those who regard is as such probably have a distorted view of what this practice entails, and a restricted view of the EP's role.

DEVELOPMENTS IN TESTING

It was because of these criticisms that so much was expected of the British Ability Scales when they were published in 1978. Up to a point there is no doubt that the authors of these scales have taken such criticisms into account. Of the twenty-four scales, at least one is designed to measure school attainments directly — a word reading test. The scales can be used independently of each other to provide a measure of a 'latent trait' and although the scores on various groups of scales can be summed to provide an overall measure of cognitive ability or IQ, the scales are intended to be used for profile analysis rather than to obtain general measures. There are three developmental scales — formal operational thinking, number concept and social reasoning — which derive from well-established psychological models. Unlike most traditional test items, these scales are based on a clear rationale and can be related to hierarchically organized curriculum objectives. As Elliot (1975) points out, the scales can be used in a criterion referenced way (to be explained later) and are not merely measures of a norm referenced kind. The scores obtained on these scales are different from those on traditional tests because:

> A scaled score may provide a deviation measure from a population norm: a developmental level describes a whole system of operations between the child and the environment which is a sufficient and complete *modus operandi* for the child at that stage. This can form a wide base on which to plan programmes and an insight into the sort of approach appropriate. (Pearson, 1975).

Elliot (1974) underpins his test construction procedures with a similar rationale to that of those who have criticized the old 'capacity' model:

> Achievement tests sample relatively narrow, acquired skills and information which children are specifically taught at school. Intelligence tests, however, frequently tap information which is acquired through incidental learning and cover a wide range of skills which are seldom taught.

These skills are conceived in traditional psychobiological terms:

> Apart from the fact that achievement tests usually do not have as *high loadings of heritabilities* (Jensen 1973) and that they usually show higher correlations with environmental variables, such as home conditions and quality of schooling than intelligence tests, the clearest point of difference is usually found in an examination of item content. (p. 314)

THE THEORETICAL BACKGROUND

As a psychometric test the BAS has much to recommend it, and is certainly an improvement on many previous tests. However, whether or not it is what practitioners really need in relation to the aforementioned school/curriculum oriented approach remains to be seen. At first sight the BAS appears to be innovative, but closer inspection suggests that certain features are still well within the traditional mould. Let us take, for example, aspects of the theoretical background indicated in the above statements by Elliot. Both these quotations reflect a position which is identical to that established by psychologists in the 1960s in their response to the sociological and political criticisms of the 1950s, and is perfectly compatible with using the WISC test, and, for that matter, the Stanford Binet. It was a position worked out to justify the use of psychometrics when the rationale on which they were previously based had been largely discredited.

According to the Plowden Report (1967, para. 64) the view held by 'most psychologists' at that time was:

> that there is no sharp distinction between measured intelligence and educational attainments. Both are the product of genetic and environmental factors: both are learned. Intelligence refers to generalized thinking powers which have developed from experience in and out of school; attainments are more directly influenced by the school curriculum.

This is not a view that even Cyril Burt would have been totally at odds with, although he would have been critical of the opening sentence. In an educational introduction under the title of 'Modern concepts of intelligence' produced as a special edition of the *Journal and Newsletter* of the Association of Educational Psychologists, C. James (1970) wrote:

> Burt, Vernon, Pidgeon and Graham . . . display unanimity in their professional approach to a gradual modification of the 'capacity theory' of education — for as Burt succinctly says 'with a few exceptions (eye colour and sociological differences of the blood) every observable characteristic is the end product of the joint action of both nature and nurture'.

The essential difference between Burt and other contributors was not in relation to the nature/nurture issue over which there was a large measure of agreement, but over the extent to which the others denied the viability of measuring genetic potential with intelligence tests. Both Graham and Vernon argued that the way intelligence tests had been distinguished from attainment tests in the past was false. According to Graham (1970):

> All that one can say is that the intelligence test aims at tapping incidental learning and more generalized thinking abilities, acquired in the less structured and total environment, whereas attainment tests attempt to describe how well a person deals with the more deliberate and systematic teaching within the educational setting. (page 56)

Vernon also agreed that the aim of these tests was to measure intellectual skills of a general kind which were affected by influences both in and out of school. He did not agree that such tests measured genetic potential, but rather were measures of educational potential:

> not because they are pure measures of Intelligence A but because a child who has developed effective schemata in his daily life thinking and behaviour, through some combination of good genes with fortunate circumstances, might normally be expected to use these in the school situation. (page 63)

Elliot's 'latent traits' and Vernon's 'effective schemata' have much in common. They are not intended to denote capacity in the Burt sense, but by implication are fundamental, generalizable and primary; they are affected by learning experiences, but are different from school attainments because they reflect skills that are not formally taught; and they have a genetic component.

In practice, the differences between the theoretical positions

Vernon and Elliot do not seem to amount to very much. Not even the most ardent advocates of the 'technology of testing' ever recognized it as constituting anything other than *part* of a psychological examination, and there has always been a concern for the cautious interpretation of scores in the light of knowledge about the probabilities of error. Thus Burt (1970) remarked in response to criticism of his approach to intelligence and its measurement in education:

> Let me repeat what I have so often stated in my published reports: if a child fails in certain tests of intelligence, that does not necessarily prove he is dull or defective, nor (in other cases) unfit for scholarship; if on the other hand he succeeds, that can almost always be taken as proof that he does possess at least the degree of ability that his answers indicate. (page 35)

ITEM CONTENT

Another feature of the BAS which is strikingly traditional is revealed in the item content of the various scales. Apart from those derived from developmental theories, and the reading test, many of them have been included because they were previously used in prestigious tests like the WISC and Binet. Tests in this category include Block Design, Comprehension, Delayed Memory, Fluency, Matrices, Naming Vocabulary, Perceptual Motor, Recall of Designs, Recall of Digits, Similarities, Speed of Problem Solving, etc.

Many of the items on these scales have a long history and some of them are similar to items on the original Binet scale. Although Binet was able to define intelligence and could theorize about intellectual development, he was a researcher very much in the 'positivist' tradition. Only some of his tests represented conscious attempts to operationally define theoretical concepts. His selection of test items was based on two criteria: (a) the proportion of passes should increase with age (b) teacher judgements of 'bright' and 'dull' children in terms of school performance. This constituted the main validity aspects of the test items. Thus a good test item was one where the percentage of passes increased from younger to older children and where there was some evidence that the item was a meaningful measure of intelligence in terms of independent criteria such as teacher ratings.

When Terman and Merrill revised the Binet Scales in 1937 a similar approach was adopted. In *Measuring Intelligence* (1937), Terman described his method of selecting items as follows:

1. A survey of the literature on the old Stanford-Binet and a study of every kind of intelligence test item that had been used or suggested.
2. The first principle was to give preference, other things being equal, to types of test items that experience had shown to yield high correlations with acceptable criteria of intelligence.
3. Practical considerations were also taken into account — time requirement, convenience of adminstation.
4. He considered that a number of tests had 'universally proved their worth', e.g. analogies, opposites, vocabulary, similarities and differences, verbal and pictorial completion, absurdities, drawing designs, memory for meaningful material and for digits.

Clearly these tests had only 'universally proved their worth' in the schooling system whence criteria for success or failure on the test were derived. As Kamin (1974, p. 226) observes: 'IQ tests, as they were designed to do, predict on a better than chance basis who will do well in the kinds of school training now employed'.

In fact it is by no means certain, that, for the purposes of EPs, IQ tests are in fact better predictors of success than some other more modest and less elaborately standardized tests. In the light of this, the inclusion of a number of traditional items can only by justified on the grounds of their providing relatively stable scores.

It is interesting that when Elliot is defending his choice of items he falls back on a similar argument to Terman, i.e., he refers to the presumed consensus about the 'worth' of the tests:

> I have no wish to go into the various reasons why these traditional sub tests are so frequently included in ability scales. I have no doubt that psychologists themselves can think of a number of reasons other than that the items yield stable scores. (1975, p. 9)

Well, can they? And, if so, what are the reasons? From what psychological theories are they derived? By what criteria are they considered to be measures of important intellectual attainments? If the developmental scales have an advantage because of the clarity of their rationale why should not this also apply to the other tests? The test constructors are silent on such matters.

RELATIONSHIP TO THE SCHOOL CURRICULUM

It will be recalled that one of the practitioner criticisms of traditional tests was their unrelatedness to the curriculum. Even if the

BAS does tap relevant areas it seems unlikely that this criticism can be adequately met. Apart from the reading test, the most likely candidates for use in a criterion referenced way are the developmental scales since it is possible that these could be related to a series of hierarchically organized curricula objectives. However, these are not detailed enough in the particular area of competence they purport to measure to provide sufficient information for remedial programmes. For example, if one were interested in a child's number skills, an *ad hoc* diagnostic number test could provide much more useful information (and more cheaply!) than the appropriate scale on the BAS. In practice one would still tend to use the BAS normatively and follow up with more curriculum specific diagnostic tests.

Of course, one could argue that what I have done here is to confuse a general with a specific test. They have a different job to do, but both are important. The general test gives an overall picture of attainments; the specific test is a follow-up test designed to provide a more detailed exploration of an area suggested by an analysis of the pattern of scores on the general test. But this — in the case of the BAS — leads us straight back to the implicit assumption that intelligence or abilities tests measure features of cognitive functioning which are allegedly fundamental, generalizable and primary. Why else choose them?

Another point is that the developmental scales will only be useful if the curriculum to which they are related is structured on the basis of similar assumptions about developmental paths in those areas. In other words, it is assumed that curriculum planners are well versed in and sympathetic towards the psychological theories of Piaget and Kohlberg. But, particularly in view of the well-known criticisms of these theories (see Phillips and Kelly, 1975; Donaldson, 1978), why should we expect curriculum planners to limit themselves in this way? The excercise seems to involve the imposition on educators of dubious psychological constructs via an 'objective' measuring instrument.

WHY RETAIN INTELLIGENCE OR ABILITIES TESTS?

Since even modern versions of the traditional intelligence test fail to answer the most serious practitioner criticisms, why should they be retained as an important part of the psychologist's 'armoury'? Some EPs, in fact, have not done so. They have relegated this form of testing to a lesser position, and attempted to develop alternative strategies which will be discussed later in this book.

Just how far these tests have been rejected by the majority of EPs, however, is difficult to estimate, and this is the subject of another chapter. But the question arises as to how it is that practitioners who largely accept the criticisms can justify giving the tests any office room at all. There seem to be two major forms of justification, one theoretical and one pragmatic.

CULTURALLY VALUED ATTAINMENTS

Some EPs feel that even if intelligence and abilities tests are not directly related to the curriculum they nevertheless provide a range of attainments which are 'culturally valued' but easily missed if tests are too closely tied to school attainment. This is similar to the theoretical position of Vernon, briefly outlined above, except that the emphasis is on the sociological rather than the psychological side of the coin. Gillham (1974) regards intelligence as a rating label which is culturally relative with respect to the content of 'behaviours' described as intelligent.

Although there is an awareness of the importance of cultural factors by these modern critics, they rarely go far enough in spelling out the implications of the 'cultural view' for appraising cognitive functioning in a school setting. The arguments are usually framed against the background of a recognition of a cultural consensus 'in our society', but the problems raised by this conception are not fully explored. For example, Gillham (1978) makes the point that 'Norms are important because, in our culture and particularly in relation to children, the dimension of age level is fundamental to our perception of whether or not a problem exists' (page 91). This is an assertion which may be true but certainly not self-evidently so. Is age, for example, as fundamental as race, sex or class? The same applies to any list of 'culturally valued attainments' that we may draw up. The implication of adopting the 'cultural view' is quite simply that we have to take this problem seriously and recognize the need for further analysis and demonstration before pointing to values about which there is a supposed consensus. The problem is made complex by the fact that 'our society' is not culturally homogeneous or at least only partly so, and is characterized by a diversity of beliefs and values relating to a variety of subcultural groupings. Even within any one culture or subculture values often appear contradictory and incompatible when viewed in isolation from the context of their application.

Another complication which needs to be taken into account

is the various interpretations of the concept of culture. Entwistle (1978) distinguishes between what he describes as a 'descriptive' from a 'normative' view of culture. The former is concerned with the description of the 'whole way of life' of a group (e.g., the products of their intellectual and artistic activity, their recreation and leisure activities, their work, etc.) or with a description of one or more parts of that totality, whereas the latter is concerned with the 'best' and most valued aspects of life either with respect to the whole or, in its narrower sense, with a part of that whole (e.g., the arts). According to Entwistle an educationally relevant concept of culture must be normative, because not all aspects of a culture may be considered to be enhancing and beneficial from an educational viewpoint: 'In the descriptive sense which includes a total way of life a culture must include strands which are technologically or economically dysfunctional, others which aggravate social injustice, and yet others which offer moral and aesthetic values' (page 110).

From this point of view all 'total ways of life' of different groups in society are cultural curates' eggs — they contain that which should be reinforced and developed by education and that which should be ignored or expunged. For example, it is wrong to celebrate *all* working class as it is to condemn all middle class values (these terms are used here as a convenient shorthand to indicate that different groups have different cultures and a fuller exposition would have to recognize the problematics of the working class/middle class distinction at the cultural and structural levels). As soon as this is recognized then a number of complex problems of interpretation present themselves when selecting intelligence test-type items supposedly reflecting culturally valued attainments. How do we interpret the valued elements of the different (regional, ethnic, social class, etc.) cultures in relation to the cultural mainstream? How much do subcultures contribute to the cultural values of the school and to what extent is this desirable? It seems that such issues have to be closely examined before one can even begin to select items which in the form of a relatively short test can reflect valued attainments. The starting point would clearly be a series of appreciative studies of the 'total way of life' of various subgroups in society. We would expect the construction of tests to be preceded by empirical studies similar to those undertaken by Labov (1973) who demonstrated that the culture of young blacks in America, despite their apparent inarticulation and poor showing on traditional tests, contained styles of thought that were readily relatable to those valued in the education system.

If a test situation is used at all, then it should be an exploratory exercise with the tester striving to appreciate the culturally located rationality of the testee. The difficulty of the exercise should not be underestimated. It is clearly not a soft option. One is reminded of Holt's (1967) statement of what understanding the child's mind involves:

> Now, if it were possible for us to look into the minds of children and see what gaps in their mental models most need filling a good case could be made out for giving them the information needed to fill them. But this is not possible. We cannot find out what children's mental models are like, where they are distorted, where incomplete. We cannot make direct contact with a child's understanding of the world. Why not? First because to a very considerable extent he is unaware of his own understanding. Secondly because he hasn't the skill to put his understanding into words, least of all words that he could be sure would mean to us what they mean to him. Thirdly, because we haven't time.

A procedure which attempted to take this outlook into account would be very different from the usual standardized test procedure with its fixed instructions and marking criteria. If commercial test material were used, it would need to be employed in a way that was more akin to a 'testing of limits' approach, i.e., one that involved going beyond the standardized instructions and therefore unscorable. It would be essentially an experimental procedure which attempted to recode the test questions so that they were closer to the child's language.

The test experimenters would concentrate on 'reassembling' the event until the child entered into the action and generated spontaneous thought processes in interaction with the tester. The approach would be open-ended and it could not be assumed that the child would confine his responses within the limits of a particular framework suggested by the tester. Such an approach was adopted by Roth (1974) using a commercially produced test — the Peabody Picture Vocabulary Test. He demonstrated that this particular test in its standardized form was inadequate for demonstrating the verbal skills of black children. He concluded that a 'probing' technique was preferred which meant that the adult had to adapt to the unexpected aspects of the child's answer as well as the child adapting to the adult. The emphasis here was on the maximization of social interaction, as opposed to its minimization as in standardized tests.

This social and phenomenologically oriented approach is apparent in the work of some EPs (see Ravenette, 1974), and implicit in some of the criticisms of those like Gillham (1974, 1978) who seek to reconstruct educational psychology. However, this does not lead to a complete rejection of testing by these authors. In Gillham's case such 'yardsticks' are necessary in order to ascertain whether or not problems exist and therefore psychometrics can have an important role to play in relation to the work of practitioners, one of whose main tasks is to assess the significance and seriousness of problems thrown up in the education system. As indicated above, what is missing here is an appreciation of the complexities of cultures and the problematic nature of 'norms'.

PSYCHOMETRICS AND PROFESSIONAL SURVIVAL

The second main reason for the retention of tests is a pragmatic one. The development of the BAS bears witness to the continuing need for an all-purpose psychometric package. It would clearly be an oversimplfication to attribute the production of such a package solely to the demands of professional survival, but it has certainly played an important part in the emergence of the profession as a distinct group with a special contribution. A number of sociological studies have demonstrated that the ideas which guide professional practices are related to how the profession perceives itself and also how it perceives itself in relation to other professional groups, (Elliot, 1973; Pettigrew, 1973).

Ideas influencing practice can be regarded as a function of the group's attempt to enhance its own interests. Thus, for example, according to Bitensky (1973) it was in the interests of social workers in America after the Second World War for the psychoanalytic model of social work practice to supersede the social action model because in a period when the new political administration had created more welfare services, an emphasis on the importance of individualistic explanations provided a 'space' for social workers to provide a useful contribution.

Similarly, it could be argued that it was in the interest of EPs in the Plowden era to argue for explanations of success and failure in school in terms of social psychological, e.g. attitudes, and to underplay the role of macro-sociological concepts, e.g. social class (see Swift, 1973).

Likewise it is in the interest of EPs to support and maintain the theory and practice of intelligence or abilities testing. This particular knowledge and skill continues to provide him with information which is directly and readily communicable to teachers, but which, potentially at any rate, adds a further dimension to routine school achievement measures. It also provides a measure of the cognitive and even emotional aspects of child development which is more precise and 'objective' than that typically obtained by doctors in a clinic situation. It provides a readily definable basis for the claim that EPs have a special contribution to make towards the appraisal of special educational needs; and for the claim that they should be key figures in SE procedures, even if they may be forced, because of their small numbers, to delegate their responsibilities to others. All this disinclines the average EP from being so critical of the principles of psychometrics that he would feel compelled to reject them outright in theory and in practice.

In general, intelligence tests are well packaged and can be presented in a way which can be readily appreciated as expertise by the consumer. They are also suitable instruments for use in a naional policy framework. As Larson (1977, p. 31) points out, in order for knowledge to be acceptable as expertise with a universal application it 'must be specific enough to impart distinctiveness to the professional "commodity", it must be formalized and codified enough to allow "standardization" of the "product" — which means ultimately, standardization of the procedures'.

Intelligence tests also help to unite the profession. Knowledge at the core of the paradigm constitutes an important aspect of professional indentity. It is vital that such knowledge is made visible to the professionals themselves and this means it needs to be clarified as 'common ground' for the less experienced as well as for the more experienced and for the relatively unsophisticated as well as the most sophisticated members of the profession.

As the same time, it has not been in his interest in terms of professional survival to become over-identified with the psychometric aspects of the traditional paradigm. At the 'edges' of the paradigm are other elements which provide support for his claim for a much broader role within education and for the claim to be different from other types of psychologists whose encroachment is not altogether unrelated to the reassertion of medical influence. If on the one hand he can claim special knowledge of universal features of cognitive development as measured by various tests, on the other he can also claim to have knowledge of specific contexts, particularly educational ones, which are crucial aspects of the environment in which the child develops. This might enable him to make more meaningful interpretations of test scores, but can also lead to a shift away from an emphasis on obtaining such scores in the first place to a primary concern with the manipulation of environmental variables supportive of the claim that he is heavily involved in 'treatment'.

THE TRADITIONAL PRACTITIONER PARADIGM

The allegiance to psychometrics can be attributed to the lack of a fully sociological critique of tests and a desire to retain a 'scientific' tool which helps to maintain professional identity. This can be seen as an aspect of a general approach to practice which can be characterized as 'traditional' — as an aspect of what I shall call the 'traditional practitioner paradigm' (see Kuhn, 1962). By practitioner paradigm I mean the common approach to practice in the light of a unified body of knowledge and skills. It implies that problems are conceptualized and resolutions sought within the confines of certain epistemological parameters and that explanations and recommendations for action based on those explanations will be of a particular type. Within the paradigm most activities are 'puzzle solving' and routine, because the range of options open to the practitioner is restricted both in terms of the questions that are allowable and the solutions which are taken seriously.

I am suggesting that the allegiance to psychometrics results from operating with a paradigm characterized by the influence of the positivist tradition in psychology and an approach to the study of social and psychological phenomena which is rooted in the doctrine of methodological individualism.

By positivism in this context is meant the methodological orientation which assumes that it is possible to make theory free observations and express these in a neutral 'scientific' language. Whether the method adopted is hypothetic-deductive or inductive, it is assumed that facts and variables can be described in a neutral manner and this is the important 'starting point' for scientific investigation, the 'bedrock' on which the theoretical structures are built (see Giddens, 1976).

The empiricist approach is a typical feature of test construction and rests heavily on the assumption that an acceptable, operational definition of ability can be arrived at relatively uncontroversially. The emphasis has been on how particular items 'work' in a given population with very little regard for why the item is worth considering in the first place. An elaborate edifice is then built upon the basis of data generated by statistical manipulations and the final form of the test has the appearance of being the result of much objective and dispassionate scientific research.

Although most positivist psychologists have considered their approach to be akin to the 'natural sciences', the latter have, in fact, largely moved away from positivism. The 'new' philosophy of science rejects positivism and empiricism. Popper's critique of induction, empiricism and positivist scientific method is well known.

He rejected the 'fact gathering' approach and advocated a hypothesis-generating innovative approach which denied pre-thoretical observation and insisted on the need for falsification rather than reification.

EPs, of course, are not the only professionals in education who like to base their practices on 'scientific evidence' (see Karier, 1976). Up to a point ideas from scientific psychology also have an affinity with the interests of teachers and administrators, but they are not as crucial for their identity as they are for the EPs'.

Another related aspect of the traditional practitioner paradigm is the doctrine of 'methodological individualism'.

Lukes (1977) argues that 'methodological individualism' makes a number of different claims ranging from those which contain propositions about which are 'most non-social' to those which are 'most social'. The most non-social are: 'propositions incorporating only predicates... about human beings as material objects and make no reference to and presuppose nothing about consciousness or any feature of any social group or institution' (page 119).

This form of explanation and two others, one involving explanations presupposing consciousness (e.g., in terms of 'aggression' or 'gratification') and the other involving minimal social reference (e.g., in terms of 'co-operation', 'power' and 'esteem') are considered by Lukes to be exclusive in the sense of ruling out of court explanations 'which appeal to social forces, structural features of society, institutional factors and so on....' (page 122). A fourth form of explanation, one that is maximally social (e.g., cashing cheques, saluting, voting) is question begging in that it 'builds crucial social factors or features of society into allegedly explanatory individuals' (page 121). It thus claims to exclude explanation in terms of social forces, social structure, etc., but, in fact, presupposes such features.

An illustration of a 'partly social' explanation is that which might be derived from Kohlberg's theory of moral development on which one of the scales of the BAS is based. This is clearly a theory which deals with social psychological phenomena, i.e., the socialization of the child with respect to 'moral' behaviour. There is, however, a central ambiguity in Kohlberg's work which is also evident in the work of other developmental psychologists like Piaget. Consciousness and experience are important but so too is the biological foundation. Phillips and Kelly (1975) argue that 'for Kohlberg as well as Piaget "massive general experience" is not enough to explain the hierarchical pattern of human development' (p. 371). In place of the idea that experiential differences account for psychological differences, Kohlberg and Piaget adopt the 'interactional' model referred to previously. 'The growing child with his developing neural machinery is interacting with his environment and is thus under going experience' (p. 373).

This ambiguity is borne of the conceptual split which in the ultimate analysis both authors make between biology and society. This often enables an assumption of biological primacy — biology is overlaid with social factors like an 'artificial' element imposed on a 'natural base'.

The introduction of biological explanations is a feature of the methodological individualistic doctrine in that such explanations entail references to individuals as entities abstracted from society and possessing 'properties' in terms of which social phenomena can be explained. The starting point of investigation is the characteristics of individuals as if these could be conceived independently of their social context. Even though the part played by this context is explicitly recognized by referring to the 'influences' of cultural and social factors, the main thrust of the investigation is to seek explanations in terms of individual differences which are prior to social origins.

Even when explanations in terms of this doctrine are 'more social' in Lukes' sense, the assumptions that influence day to day practice are informed by presuppositions about social structure and social forces only in a way that does not impinge on routine decision making. Mostly they are concerned with 'causes' emanating from individuals who possess certain attitudes and perceptions which may or may not be related to an interactive context but which are usually not seen as determined (even in a weak, nondeterminist sense) by wider structural aspects.

Sociology is usually criticized by methodological individualists for not taking the individual into account. Even when sociologists do attempt to explain individual motivation, their statements are considered to be derived from remote structural analyses which are more a reflection of their own personal construct systems than an accurate account of 'meanings' for the individuals they are supposed to be studying. Or in the 'less social' version of the doctrine these structural analyses impose a view of human beings which ignores the 'facts' of biological individual differences.

Structural analyses at the macro level, however, do not necessarily rule out the contributions of individuals in an interactive context at the micro level even though such considerations constitute a problematic for such analyses. But the reverse is not true of methodological individualism which insists on outlawing explanations that cannot be reduced to facts about invidivuals.

It is this theoretically narrow approach which Lukes considers to be the main deficiency of the doctrine.

In summary, the doctrines of positivism and methodological individualism preclude any serious analysis of alternative social arrangements because they lead to an approach to the study of psychological and educational phenomena which takes the prevailing social and political forces for granted and assumes that analyses in these social terms are to be ruled out of court.

THE EXPERT ROLE

In this chapter an attempt has been made to analyse a 'core' aspect of the knowledge base — psychometrics — and to assess the extent to which recent developments in abilities testing have been a satisfactory response to practitioner criticisms. The continued allegiance to psychometrics results from the lack of an adequate critique and the desire to retain a particular professional identity, both of which are related to the pervasiveness of a traditional practitioner paradigm. This paradigm has dominated the practice of educational psychology from the earliest years. The key elements of this paradigm are a particular brand of academic psychology characterized by positivism and methodological individualism. This provides the 'scientific' knowledge which is the basis of the EP's special contribution and thus of his expertise.

Expertise based on 'science' is the most prestigious form of expertise and therefore a paradigm which derives from a psychology which claims to be scientific is not likely to be rejected without serious consideration. Educational psychologists have been reluctant therefore to break with the paradigm which continues to be a pervasive influence on practice in modern times.

The EP working within the traditional paradigm is typically a cautious expert. Most statements about his contribution have been framed in a way that plays down the expert role. As Vernon (1950) put it:

> Educational psychology is in many respects an advanced and highly technical form of applied science. Owing to the nature of the material with which it deals, it is more comparable to medicine than, say, physical engineering. Hence its present status in education is a humble one; it cannot by itself give answers to definite questions about the art of teaching. Still less can it affirm the soundness of educational policies or ideals. The psychologist, when asked for the answer to any educational problem should admit this and should realise that his own judgement is often no

better or even poorer than that of the parent, the teacher or the administrator who have consulted him. (pages 29—30)

Nevertheless, the cautiouness of the EP's approach should not blind us to the fact that he is claiming expertise in certain crucial areas. As the same author went on to say: 'Educational psychology has established a number of important conclusions regarding mental qualities and attainments, their measurements, inter-relations, their distributions etc. about selection, guidance, teaching materials and methods' (page 30).

It is this splitting of 'conclusions', i.e. facts, from 'judgement', i.e. value judgement, that enables EPs working within the traditional paradigm to project an image of caution, humility and aloofness in relation to the educational controversies of the day while at the same time claiming to be making an impartial contribution based on expertise which in fact prejudges many of the issues.

CHAPTER 4

Knowledge in practice: a questionnaire and interview study

In the previous chapter an attempt was made to outline and appraise the main features of the traditional practitioner paradigm and to provide an explanation of its continued appeal among practitioners despite the various criticisms. It was assumed throughout that the traditional approach was in fact an approach to practice adopted by most EPs and was the dominant orientation in the profession as a whole. However, in view of the various attempts in recent years to develop different forms of practice it seems reasonable to ask whether or not it is the case that the average EP of today continues to follow a traditional path and, if not, in what other directions might he be moving? To this end a two-part empirical study was conducted involving a questionnaire on professional knowledge and face to face interviews with a number of practising EPs.

THE QUESTIONNAIRE STUDY

The questionnaire aimed to provide information on two aspects of the traditional paradigm, namely the commitment to the technology of testing and the reliance on esoteric knowledge derived mainly from a psychology with a positivist and individualist orientation (see Appendix 2). The items were chosen with regard to certain assumptions about their relationship to the traditional paradigm and framed with certain expectations in mind as to the kind of responses that might be obtained.

It was assumed that a list of items referring to tests in use would give an indication of the extent of involvement in the technology of testing. 'Deep' involvement would be indicated by the proportion of respondents admitting to using tests regularly. It was also assumed that if respondents were not test oriented this would be revealed and that they would indicate their reasons in the space provided. Since one of the researcher's aims was to investigate the existence of 'alternatives', respondents' comments on why they did not use tests would be particularly interesting. As for the esoteric knowledge of the traditional paradigm, it was assumed that a commitment here would be indicated by responses:

(a) to a list of perspectives ranging from 'hard-nosed' experimental psychology to historical materialism and sociology;
(b) to a list of psychologists representing various schools of psychology and different theoretical orientations;
(c) to a list of educationalists most of whom were based in disciplines other than psychology;
(d) to a question about general reading;
(e) to a list of journals;
(f) to a question about psychological research.

It was assumed that the extent of allegiance to the traditional paradigm would be shown by the rank order list of preferences on the four lists provided and by comparing the rank order of the different lists. The responses to questions on reading and research would be interpretable as supportive or not as the case may be of the traditional paradigm.

In 1978, the questionnaires were sent to all the principal or chief educational psychologists of all the local education authorities in England and Wales with an accompanying letter (see Appendix 1) explaining the purpose of the questionnaire and asking them to forward it to any of their staff (EPs only) who wished to co-operate in the research. As a result, 291 completed questionnaires were returned representing approximately one-third of all practising EPs.

A serious problem with such a response rate is that the respondents may not be representative of the population and this has to be taken into account when interpreting the results. There is no way in which this problem can be completely overcome. An attempt was made to contact a number of non-respondents (N = 16) and on interview there was no indication that this small group would have differed markedly in their responses from the majority of respondents. Another possibility is to discriminate between late and early respondents on the assumption that the former are more likely to share characteristics with non-respondents. Two groups were compared, and there were no obvious differences between them.

TESTS

A list of twenty-five well-known tests was provided and respondents were asked to indicate if they used a test regularly, occasionally, hardly ever or not at all. The respondent was informed that he could add other tests, and space was provided for this. The percentage of the total number of respondents who fell into each category was calculated for each test, and rank orders obtained for regular usage and combined usage i.e., regular plus occasional (see Appendix 3). It is clear from these figures that although most respondents admitted to using a reasonably wide range of tests on an occasional or regular basis there was a tendency for them to use some tests considerably more than others. The figures for regular use suggest that the WISC, an individual intelligence test, is clearly the most used test. This is followed by an individual test of reading ability, another individual intelligence test and then a shorter individual test of reading attainment.

The WISC is a test which is consonant with the rationale of the traditional paradigm. It attempts to measure abilities of universal significance and provide an 'objective' assessment.

Within the traditional paradigm in the context of its application to SE an important aspect of the assessment procedure has always been to provide information on current attainment in basic educational skills, particularly reading, and then to compare this with intelligence test scores. The Neale appears to have superseded the Burt and Schonell as the most used reading test. Unlike these two, it is not solely a word recognition test consisting of a number of isolated words on a card but a series of paragraphed passages which the testee can read for meaning. The child is tested for comprehension and there are a number of simple diagnostic tests of word attack skills.

In general, the percentages indicate the kind of diagnostic sequence that one might expect of an EP working in the traditional manner: an intelligence test followed by a reading test followed perhaps by a further assessment of language skills and/or perceptual motor skills.

In addition to tests in actual use, respondents were also asked to indicate anticipated use of the British Ability Scales with the following results:

	% (rounded)
Almost certainly on a regular basis	45
Possibly on a regular basis	20
Almost certainly only occasionally	8
Possibly only occasionally	11

| I shall rarely use the BAS | 4 |
| I shall not be using the BAS at all | 2 |

This result suggested that a substantial number of EPs intend using the BAS. This may mean that the WISC might be relegated to a lesser position in terms of regular use. On the other hand, if the history of the use of the Stanford-Binet is anything to go by (according to the above rank order it is the third most used test), the WISC is likely to be used fairly regularly for some time to come, even if the BAS does eventually come to be regarded as the main test.

As we have seen, despite some innovations, the BAS is essentially in the tradition of intelligence testing and therefore represents a development within the traditional paradigm rather than a break from it. These figures suggest that testing is still an important part of the EPs' identity and that the kinds of tests relied on heavily in the past continue to be used regularly in the present and are likely to continue being used in the future.

Only two respondents indicated thay they did not use psychometric tests at all (this did not include a few principals who tended to spend most of their time on administration). This was in response to an open-ended question about the reasons for not using tests. The question was intended to provide data on 'minority' rather than 'majority' trends in the hope that this might indicate an incipient shift from the previous model.

However, apart from these two, there were no others who totally rejected intelligence testing on epistemological or any other grounds. Most of them used tests occasionally. A few were regular WISC users who qualified this by indicating that psychometric testing took up an increasingly smaller proportion of their time. Most of the comments revolved around the issue of 'relevance'. Psychometric testing was not thought to be particularly useful in understanding the problems with which EPs were typically faced. They failed to provide data which could be meaningfully related to the classroom and were not obviously and directly helpful in planning educational programmes.

> They are limited in range and scope and often tap a few often irrelevant areas. Provide no adequate basis for future work with the child. Insufficiently related to classroom acvitivies. (R19)

> Most of the important questions about people, child development, families can be asked without recourse to objective standardised testing. (R34)

> Norm referenced tests have some predictive value, they have no

prescriptive value regarding the curriculum. I'm in the business of treatment, so I should not need to use tests so frequently. (R113)

Psychometric tests which focus on a level of functioning or measure a specific disability are useless unless they have definable educational/remedial implications. (R147)

Mainly because of their irrelevance to the problem situations with which I am involved in my work. Also because they take up a lot of time which may be spent more usefully. (R208)

A small number were concerned about the consequences of testing, particularly the negative aspects of 'labelling' and the tendency for others to misinterpret or misuse findings.

I have become convinced that aside from consideration of utility to psychologists, the reporting of results produces inevitable and undesirable consequences through the reification and over generalisation which takes place amongst other groups. (R207)

... [concerned with] the effects they have on teacher perception of child and expectations. (R40)

Alternative approaches suggested included non-standardized individual techniques, observation methods, curriculum-related assessment and criterion referenced approaches. Some of these alternatives were, in fact, already included on the list of tests. Thus R37 felt that:

Norm referenced assessment rarely adds much to problem assessment. Rep grids and observation say more about behavioural and attitudinal aspects, micro-learning and criterion-referenced say more about learning difficulties.

To what extent do these comments suggest a potential break with the traditional paradigm? As far as most of the commentators were concerned, if such a break were imminent it did not, for the moment at any rate, mean a complete rejection of psychometrics since most of them still used intelligence tests. Despite the fact that psychometrics were thought to be irrelevant to many current pragmatic concerns, e.g., making detailed recommendations on the basis of curriculum-related assessment, they nevertheless were considered by some critics to have a predictive value which might prove useful in other aspects of the work.

Perspectives

In the next section respondents were asked about their preferences— 'strong' or weak'—in relation to various perspectives in psychology.

In this and the next three sections the researcher was hoping to obtain information about the range and nature of the theoretical knowledge drawn upon in day to day practice.

These particular perspectives were chosen because they seemed to represent schools of psychology which traditionally had influenced practice. A number of perspectives were included which were outside this framework, e.g., 'historical materialism' and 'sociological'. Space was provided for the respondent to add other perspectives if he wished to do so. Rank order lists were obtained for the strongly preferred category and for the combined 'strong' and 'weak' categories (see Appendix 3).

Most respondents seemed to adopt a generally favourable attitude to developmental, behaviourist and eclectic perspectives and also, though to a lesser extent, to psychometric, cognitive and experimental. The sociological perspective had substantial general support, but was clearly not among the most popular.

It was felt that 'strong' responses, since they perhaps reflected more emotional and intellectual involvement, should be regarded as more crucial in relation to practice and therefore should be given more 'weight' in interpretation. Thus, eclecticism seems to represent the dominant perspective, which is supported, in a sense, by the fact that the next two in order of 'strong' preference, the developmental and behaviourist, can both themselves be construed as being more like eclectic umbrella terms than, say, symbolic interactionism or psychoanalysis.

Another interesting feature is the pattern of negative responses. This was the only section of the questionnaire where the respondents were asked to indicate a negative attitude. The 'x' was not, in fact, widely used, which is scarcely surprising for a group who strongly favoured eclecticism, and only very small numbers were negatively inclined to only a few perspectives. However, the one exception to this was psychoanalysis towards which 29% of the total group expressed a negative attitude. Many of these included respondents who claimed to be eclectic as well as a disproportionate number of those strongly preferring the behaviourist perspective. For a small minority of EPs, therefore, the traditional tension between behaviourism and psychoanalysis still appeared to be there. It is mentioned here because it is really the only tension detected among respondents between schools of psychology. This again gives support to the prevalence of the eclectic view. The data, however, are difficult to interpret because so much depends on what respondents took to be the meanings of the terms used. The researcher could clearly be accused of attempting to impose his own constructs on the researched. The only check against this was in the way the material for the questionnaire was selected. It was decided that, if items of this type were to be included at all, assumptions would have to be made about the typical meaning of an item for practising EPs. These assumptions were made after discussions with EPs before and after the pilot study and after consulting the various journals that were thought to be popular among practitioners, i.e., the AEP *Journal*, the BPS *Bulletin* and the *British Journal of Educational Psychology* which in fact approximated to the rank order actually obtained.

Other items were included which it was felt would be familiar to EPs who were attempting to break from the traditional paradigm, e.g., sociological and historical materialism.

Psychologists and educationalists

Respondents were asked to indicate which on a list of thirty-three psychologists and a separate list of thirty educationalists they had consciously and deliberately drawn on as a resourse in their day to day practice. Rank order lists were drawn up for regular and combined usage (see Appendix 3).

In view of the popularity of the developmental and behaviourist perspectives it is not surprising that Skinner and Piaget are at the top of the lists, and we would also expect eclectic practitioners to refer to a fairly wide range of psychologists, which they clearly do, even if only occasionally. A striking feature is that none of the top six are typically associated with the psychmetric tradition, although it is important to bear in mind that Piaget-based items have been incorporated in the BAS. It is possible that this, in conjunction with the responses on test usage, could be interpreted as reflecting the professional dilemma of being obliged to use tests, but not wishing to be over-identified with them.

The list of educationists contained the names of a wide range of well known authors in the field. Most of them, though not all, e.g., Dewey, could be meaningfully distinguished from the psychologists on the grounds that they were primarily associated with other disciplines such as sociology, politics, history and philosophy. Certainly all the authors on this list had made contributions to the educational literature, which was not true of all the psychologists. It is interesting that the most chosen educationist — A. E. Tansley — is psychologically oriented and is therefore not typical of this group as a whole. The work of this author is directly related to one of the essential aspects of the practitioner paradigm: the diagnosis and assessment of children with special educational needs.

The next two in rank order — Bernstein and Hargreaves — are both sociologists, although the latter has probably more claim to be a social psychologist. It is possible that Bernstein relates to the emphasis in the post-Plowden era on what EPs would describe as the environmentalist view of language development. The notion of compensation for linguistic deprivation in the early years would fit with an interactional view of growth and development in infancy. There has certainly been a tendency for EPs to stress the importance of language stimulation in infancy and early childhood, while at the same time recognizing the influence of genetic factors.

Hargreaves, whose name is usually linked with the 'labelling perspective', is often regarded as having something significant to say about the role of the educational psychologist as a constructor of deviant identities. At a time when there is a great deal of talk about the integration of handicapped pupils with their colleagues in the ordinary school, Hargreaves' work is considered to be particularly pertinent. Since EPs have traditionally been associated with the 'normalization' of deviance and the swing from the medical model, it is probably not surprising that they refer to Hargreaves.

However, if we compare this list with the previous one, respondents clearly make less regular and occasional use of the educationists than they do of psychologists. Bernstein only achieves par with someone like Bowlby, and Hargreaves with Wolpe, and neither compares with psychologists like Skinner or Piaget.

Respondents seemed to feel more involved with psychology and psychology-based educational theory than with more general aspects of educational thought associated with other disciplines. In terms of the ideas they bring to practice it may reflect a tendency to describe and explain educational events in individualistic terms rather than social terms, although, as has been noted, this does not rule out the occasional explicit reference to relevant sociological concepts.

Reading

Respondents were asked to name any books and/or articles on education, psychology or related disciplines which they had read in the past year and which had made a significant impact on their professional practice. Nearly a third failed to respond at all to this question and roughly 14% either did not think any book or article had made a significant impact, e.g., 'nothing in the past year', 'nothing in particular', or 'none', or considered that there were far too many to list or thought that the question was too dificult to answer in the terms in which it was expressed, e.g., 'several which have increased my understanding but none that have changed my practice significantly' and '... difficult to relate source to subsequent impact'.

Most of the responses referred to books and articles which seemed to be in the general area of the assessment and remediation of problems (80% approximately), although obviously not all titles could be readily categorized. Those who fell into this major category referred to books and articles on different types of therapy, remedial educational programmes and teaching approaches as well as on various methods of diagnosis and assessment of learning difficulties and other educational and psychological 'handicaps'. There were a number of references specifically to behaviour modification and behaviour therapy (approximately 40% of all those on 'treatment') and some on various forms of psychotherapy, e.g., derived from humanistic psychology and family therapy.

The remaining 20% (approximately) were a miscellaneous collection of books or articles on child development, psychology, e.g., the works of Jung, educational psychology, the sociology of education (particularly the interactionist approach), philosophy and methodology and various government reports, such as Court and Taylor.

In general, most reading seemed in some way or another to be related to maladjustment and behaviour problems on the one hand and learning and educational difficulties on the other with odd references to specific handicaps like spina bifida, autism, partial hearing, partial sightedness and exceptional groups like gifted children. The sort of books popular in this area were Rutter's *Helping Troubled Children*, Raybould and Leach's *Learning and Behaviour Difficulties in School*, Mittler's *Psychological Assessment of Mental and Physical Handicaps* and those based on research at the Hester Adrian Centre.

Thus, although respondents indicated in previous sections that they had preferences for certain perspectives and particular theoreticians, in the main their reading was more obviously related to pragmatic concerns than to 'theory'. It is probable that most of these books had an eclectic theoretical backdrop, but one's impression was that books with a definite bias to behavioural psychology were well presented.

Journals

Question 8 was concerned with the frequency with which various journals were consulted — regularly, occasionally, hardly ever or not at all? A list of twenty journals was provided and this could be augmented if the respondent wished to do so (see Appendix 3).

Since most of the respondents were members of the AEP and the BPS, it is not really surprising that the *Journal* and the *Bulletin* are regularly consulted by over half of them and that over 80% consulted them either regularly or occasionally. As members, respondents would receive copies regularly through the post. Both contain articles about general matters in psychology as well as professional matters, though the *Journal* has more articles relating specifically to the work of psychologists in education. Recent editions of the *Journal* have included many articles on the role of the educational psychologist, and a substantial number on behaviour modification techniques. It usually has a section on research articles which are mainly concerned with the application of certain theoretical frameworks and methodological techniques to problems in education, but there are few articles which critically discuss the role of theory in practice or the problematics of different theoretical positions. The most frequently chosen academic journal, the *British Journal of Educational Psychology* tends to contain articles derived from research studies in the traditional mould of orthodox educational psychology.

The Times Educational Supplement seems to represent the main source of knowledge about current issues in education. This was many times more popular than either the specialist educational journals with a practical bent, such as *Remedial Education* or research journals like *Educational Research.*

A number of radical journals were included as well as the *British Journal of Sociology* to assess the significance of certain 'minority' interests, but most of these had virtually no regular consultation and only a small number of respondents consulted them even occasionally.

Research

Approximately 60% of respondents gave a straight or qualified 'yes' to the question: are you optimistic that future research in psychology will produce findings which will make a positive and significant contribution towards solving some of the more persistent educational problems? This may be supportive of the traditional paradigm in so far as it reflects the positivist's faith in the importance of applied scientific research for social amelioration.

For some of those who were more pessimistic the fact that academic research was remote from practical issues was considered the main problem. Suggested reasons for this were that academics were too concerned with esoteric theories, relied too much on the experimental tradition instead of locating research in the context of its application and based too much of their research activity on problems thrown up by previous research, with the implication that psychological research tended to be an 'incestuous' inward-looking activity. The following comments were typical:

> My feeling is that much of educational research which is carried out is not sufficiently practical in its orientation. (R25)

> No; research in psychology is geared mainly towards solving problems thrown up by previous research etc. Until academic psychologists begin to concern themselves with real problems in the real world I do not feel optimistic. (R65)

> ... experimental and academic research hasn't done much so far ... action research in the field might get us somewhere. (R59)

None of these criticisms are directed at the importance of research as such; others, however, question whether research is the key to positive educational changes.

> No — or only partially — many of our persistent educational problems require social change which is unlikely to be markedly affected by psychological research. (R6)

> No. Not a research problem — a problem of organisation and resources, i.e., politics and finance. (R9)

> No. The knowledge to deal with most problems already exists. The difficulties lie more in the availability (non-availability) of resources, poor quality of training of teachers, educational psychologists, etc. and cultural and political factors in society. (R56)

The main problem, as seen here, is more to do with the inability of the education system to apply research findings that do exist. There is a feeling among some of this group that psychological knowledge is not really being used by schools. The reasons for this are various. Some saw it as a function of the prevailing political and economical climate — changes based on research were always bedevilled by the lack of resources or by the unwillingness of political masters to go along with them. Others explained the situation in terms of the attitudes of teachers and adminstrators who blocked and frustrated changes in the directions indicated by research. Educational psychologists were also at fault, according to some commentators, not so much because of their attitude as their inability to keep up with research.

THE INTERVIEW STUDY

This part of the study involved interviews with nine local authority EPs all woking in the same School Psychological Service. The aim was basically the same as that of the questionnaire: to find out to what extent practitioners were still working with the traditional paradigm. It was hoped that this alternative method would produce data supportive of the findings of the questionnaire study and perhaps help to clarify and illuminate the varieties of meanings 'behind' some of the responses. In addition, it was felt that such an approach was necessary in order to explore the consciousness of practitioners in greater depth in those areas which were not amenable to investigation by a questionnaire, e.g., implicit assumptions about the educational context.

Initially, it was intended that the practitioners interviewed would all be working for a School Psychological Service which was not atypical with respect to the kind of work routinely undertaken by EPs and the orientation of the LEA in which it was situated. In practice, it proved impossible to obtain sufficiently detailed prior information about services (which were accessible to the researcher) to enable him to make a judgement about typicality with any degree of precision. The service eventually selected was probably atypical in that, as it eventually transpired, the majority of the EPs interviewed were attempting to work in a way which they construed as *not* traditional even if they did not necessarily regard themselves as radically oriented. In the event, the bias of the sample proved to have some advantages because data were produced on alleged alternatives to the traditional paradigm.

Each EP was interviewed individually for about an hour and the interviews were recorded on tape. The researcher began the interview by asking the interviewee to elaborate on his questionnaire responses and at a later stage introduced other topics.

Attitudes to testing intelligence and abilities

It was clear from their responses that many of the EPs did not regard testing as constituting a central aspect of their work, but nevertheless none of them objected in principle to using intelligence or ability tests. Psychologist (A) felt that there was something of a contradiction in her position on this issue. She did not use tests reguarly. She was not particularly interested in using tests because she felt there were more productive ways of spending time with a child and yet she did use them occasionally, particularly if she wanted to obtain a specific bit of information about a child, such as the vocabulary level of an unforthcoming child. The practical situation was so complex — EPs were working 'with certain environments with a lot of pressures and different attitudes and expectations' and it was almost impossible to be consistent in terms of one particular theory or model. Thus she did not like doing tests 'but I still do them once in a while ... I mean, its something quite contradictory really, but that's the way it seems to be ... and I don't seem to be able to do much about it'.

Others were fully aware of some of the dangers of being identified with intelligence tests. Psychologist (C), for example, was concerned about the expectations of other professions and how events were construed because of his existence. He quoted examples of families being stigmatized because they did not agree to a referral to the psychologist. He felt powerless to stop this and to some extent felt that he was being used. A good example was IQ testing. 'The reification of the concept by other professionals was always a possibility' and in his experience this frequently occurred.

The expectations of others that they would do tests was certainly a significant factor for most of the EPs. When Respondent (E) reached for a test, he did so in the knowledge that if other professionals saw him testing then this would be evidence for them that he was 'doing something about the problem'. Respondent (G) recognized the value of testing as a means of 'establishing some credibility' before moving into more controversial areas, implying that his psychometric role was more readily accepted by teachers than any other role.

Such expectations were likely to make more impact on a young and/or inexperienced EP than on a more mature and experienced one. He felt that although he used tests frequently he did so less than he used to: 'I think as you progress as a psychologist you build up an expertise ... you reduce your reliance on tests'. (A) considered that EPs who were at an early stage in their careers or who were just starting out tended to make more use of tests than older and more experienced psychologists, perhaps because they needed a 'crutch'. (A) also thought that in the initial stages of their careers, many young EPs were still themselves under the impression that testing was the central part of the job.

However, it would be incorrect to give the impression that these respondents did not think testing had some value and were purely constrained to use them by the expectations of others. Only one respondent, (I), said that he had given up using tests completely 'because tests were just irrelevant to the sort of questions I was wanting to ask'. Most used them either regularly or occasionally to obtain what they considered to be useful information. Respondent (B) admitted to spending a great deal of his time testing because of his particular orientation. At one time or another he would obtain some indication of the range of skills sampled by tests of most children referred to him and considered himself to be a regular user of the WISC(R). He felt that this was because he was placement oriented in his work and therefore tended to use tests because he made a large number of decisions involving changes of school. (D) said that he used individual tests to sample a broad range of skills to see how general a learning problem might be.

Even respondents, who did not use tests regularly and saw themselves as moving towards a different model of practice, tended to regard intelligence and abilities tests as providing a valid measure of a range of cognitive skills. Thus (C), who regarded himself primarily as a behavioural change agent, did not consider there was anything inherently wrong with intelligence testing as an applied psychological technique and found it useful to have a 'box of bits' providing a sample of a range of skills and for making comparisons with other children. He also considered them useful for predicting success in the education system.

Another popular reason for using tests among those who did not necessarily use them frequently was the framework they afforded when making an initial contact with a child. (F) used tests to 'structure time in interviews' and 'to get the feel of the child', which he felt he could not do by observing him/her in the classroom and listening to what other people had to say about him/her. He felt that a test was a useful way to open an interview. By the end of the test procedure both child and psychologist were fairly relaxed. He thought that children usually enjoyed doing the test because they liked sitting down and playing games with an adult. The test enabled the psychologist to be in 'a much better position to talk about what you want to talk about to teachers'. (G) also regarded the testing procedure as a useful way of structuring an interview:

> It's a structured interview and you're familiar with it and the kids' reaction to it. You can get a fair amount of information in a short

time. It would, of course, be preferable to spend more time with the kids in a more normal environment, observing and talking but given that that can't be and you want some direct information quickly, you use tests.

This respondent, like most of the others, considered that, apart from the 'spin off' effect of assisting interview strategies, the actual quantitative data obtained from tests were, in certain circumstances, useful. Like others, however, he was wary about releasing figures that could be misunderstood.

It was on the quantitative aspects of testing that most ambivalence was revealed. Some respondents who used tests to establish rapport, structure interviews and gain an impression of skills did not necessarily bother to score tests or arrive at figures which they would be willing to put in a written report or give orally to a third party. Testing was just part of a diagnostic procedure. (F) made use of quantitative data when it suited him: 'you can go back to the teacher and say look you said he was slow but he's quite bright'. Sometimes a test result can be used as an administrative lever to get things moving. If this involved 'violating' tests he was not too concerned if in general it was helpful to the child. Nevertheless, there was a moral problem involved. Likewise, if he was ever in a position where he was compelled to provide information about test performance in a situation where he felt the best interests of the child were not being served, then he would 'judge the issue and use categories instead of scores'.

The question of morality in relation to testing was also raised by Respondent (C). As far as he was concerned there was no need to be dishonest or 'fiddle' the results because you could 'always play the game of using ranges of confidence and complex statistics', i.e., to obtain a result which would create a favourable expectation of the child. Both this respondent and the previous one were certainly not test oriented, but felt that tests could be used in a way which was or seemed to be beneficial for the child. Respondent (I) was the only one to doubt that even such uses were ultimately of any value. He felt that there was no point in demonstrating how competent a child was on intelligence tests, when the problem was that he/she was not doing well on the tasks the teacher wanted him/her to do well on.

Another reason for using tests was mentioned by one respondent and implied by several others. (C) considered that many EPs continued to use tests because it was less stressful. They felt that it was possible to develop alternative ways of working, but EPs were often forced into using their time inefficiently by the context of their employment. 'So much emotional hassle takes up time and energy, coping with the bureaucracy...' EPs who wanted a quiet life turned a blind eye to these problems and adopted the less stressful test-giving model which he had largely rejected and as a consequence felt that he had more of his time taken up with worry.

Attitudes to esoteric knowledge

Most respondents drew a distinction between 'common sense' and 'knowledge from research and psychological theory'. As practitioners they had to make decisions based on what knowledge was available to them. Sometimes this was recognizable as esoteric knowledge; at others, although such knowledge may have been influential, they perceived it more as 'insight' or 'common sense'. Esoteric knowledge, however, did play a definite role in their practice. Some felt that it had helped to mould their personal conceptual frameworks. Respondent (A) said that sometimes she was not conscious of using the work of well-known psychologists, but supposed that she must be using some of their ideas, because she had read them in the past and it was likely that the ideas had filtered through to her practice. (D) said: 'Things one has already acquired eventually become part of your perceptual framework — they are at the back of your mind'.

The most common attitude of respondents was to regard esoteric knowledge as a resource which they could draw upon to assist them in decision making. Although most regarded themselves as eclectic, the actual nature of theories and research mentioned was quite limited in range. The theories referred to were mainly psychological and there were few references to sociological theories or other education theories. (C) said that if anything his allegiance was to a behaviourist perspective but in a rather loose way — he was not interested in causes but only in immediate questions such as 'Where do we go from here?' However, he did not rule out other models, such as psychometric, and used them where it was appropriate to do so. (D), although drawing on a personal conceptual framework influenced 'historically' by theories, also spent a great deal of time in a conscious effort to apply recognizable theory and research to practice. He adopted different approaches depending on the needs of the situation — a behavioural/managerial approach with 'naughty' children in the primary school and perhaps a Rogerian approach in a one to one situation with older children. He used psychological theories in 'fairly crude blocks' and 'bits' were used rather than the whole theory. He used Rogers frequently, but sometimes relied on the Freudian notion of defence mechanism. In general, he tended to favour a non-directive approach: 'I might have my own hypothesis but I'd rather it came from the client'. Although he regarded himself as eclectic, he was not conscious of deliberately juggling with a number of models all at once. He tended to concentrate on one approach, say behaviour modification, until he felt he understood it fully and could communicate it to teachers, and then perhaps he would move on to something else. Respondent (E) was not conscious of employing an elaborate framework, but worked with a concept of 'normality' derived from psychological theory and research. (F) recognized that EPs used a variety of perspectives in their work. Some used a programme-oriented, highly structured behaviourist approach and made it work because they believed in it, others functioned within what was a more humanistic or phenomenological framework. As for himself, 'I vary it a lot . . . if I get bored with one approach I change it'. He was conscious that all the approaches he used, e.g., learning theory, Kelly, Berne, might be part of a common system — a 'big meta theory'. Theories could and should be integrated. 'If you look at a Skinnerian response it's fairly obvious that the same stimulus will be interpreted differently by different people at different times . . . that's where Kelly comes in'.

Not all the respondents could be described as eclectic. At least two gave the impression of being followers of particular schools of psychology — (I) tended towards Rogerian humanistic psychology and (H) favoured a behavioural approach. But neither could be described as 'hard line'.

There was a marked tendency for many respondents to distinguish in positivist fashion between a realm of knowledge called 'theory' and a realm called 'fact'. This was typically expressed by referring to knowledge of 'what was actually happening' as opposed to what theoretically was supposed to happen and tended to be associated either with descriptions influenced by behavioural psychology or psychology with a biological/developmental orientation. (C)'s attitude referred to above was indicative of this. He did not focus on 'causes', i.e., explanations in terms of theories, but on immediate questions like 'Where do we go from here?' as if this could be stated in a theory-free way — as 'fact'. (D) used behaviourist theories, but claimed not to be a behaviourist, his main concern being merely to structure situations. Although (F) used a number of different theories, he was rather ambivalent about using theories at all. 'I very much go along with Skinner in not having theories ... don't bother with theories look at what's happening'. (G) often used a behavioural approach which to him meant making careful records and carrying out detailed observations of behaviour, and looking at 'what is actually happening, not your opinion as to what you think is happening or what you feel is happening ... but what is actually happening'.

Respondent (E) also used the phrase 'what was actually happening' in the context of an approach to practice which relied on a concept of 'normality' which did not appear to be recognized as theory bound. He felt that it was often the case that his role was to define situations in terms of 'normality' when the school was asking questions about deviant behaviour. For example, in one case: 'The question being asked was was it some kind of madness or derangement; did the child have a genuine inability to perceive that what she was doing was not normal and should therefore steps be taken to treat this?' His concept of normality was essentially biological. Children did or did not have 'intact adaptive mechanisms' and the school did or did not provide 'artificial constraints' which were incompatible with these natural processes. In fact 'in the great majority of referrals there is nothing fundamentally amiss, i.e., the individuals concerned are in some state of adaptation to the environment which is consistent with continuing to get by, and a lot of problems are generated by putting on top of that the requirements of institutions — the schools'. This respondent also evinced an ambivalence about the role of theory in practice. He felt there was an enormous gulf between the academic world and the world of psychological practice.

There was evidence here of a contradiction which was also implicit in many of the other respondents' reflections on their practice. (E) considered that there was a distinction between esoteric theory and common sense knowledge, and that if anything the latter was superior to the former. Although he felt it was useful occasionally to quarry in the literature, when dealing with most of the problems that came his way there was 'a better model out here and that's life ... in the way we normally experience it'. Only when 'common sense intuitions and normal processes' were not providing solutions did 'psychology' become necessary. However, bearing in mind (E)'s views on normality, 'natural' adaptive mechanisms and the 'artificiality' of social institutions it seems that his common sense view of reality, of 'what is actually happening', is conceived in neutral, theory-free terms and contains references to biological universals consistent with the positivist approach of the traditional paradigm. There are normal, neutral biologically-based, psychological processes which he considers to be 'fact' and therefore already embedded in his common sense knowledge.

For another respondent a similar assumption was made about the findings of various surveys on features of child development. That these might be dependent on value-loaded presuppositions of what to expect of children at various ages and stages did not deter (H) from referring to such surveys as providing useful pieces of factual information: 'because if I'm presented with a problem, particularly a behaviour problem, then I like to find out how common it is . . . '

Attitudes to expertism

Nearly all respondents rejected what they described as 'the expert role'. (E) considered that he always attempted to approach teachers in a non-expert manner. If teachers did attempt to construe him as an expert with special skills and techniques from which could be derived ready-made solutions to problems, he tried to 'knock that idea down immediately'. (H) regarded teachers' expectations in this respect as 'one of the biggest hassles of the job . . . You are regarded as an expert who can supply an answer in every situation . . . '

The notion of 'expert' clearly had negative connotations. It was associated with someone claiming to have a monopoly of superior knowledge, such knowledge being that which was derived from objective research findings. Against this was the assertion that a great deal of knowledge that EPs used in the job could not be described as superior. It was just knowledge which had accumulated as a result of being in a certain place at a certain time, of carrying out a particular function and of having certain experiences. Thus (B) distinguished between special knowledge and special role and considered that if he did not always possess the former, he usually played the latter in that he clearly had a specific job to do which nobody else did. (C) expressed the view that it was difficult for him to pinpoint exactly how he used 'psychology' because everything depended so much on local conditions and local relationships. (A) considered that she only functioned fifty per cent of her time as an 'applied scientist'. (D) considered that the EP did have a special contribution which had been recognized in Circular 2/75 and as a result of this he now felt professionally bound to fill in the appropriate form. However, the special contribution was not a 'watertight thing'. He could not say that he possessed certain knowledge of a particular kind about every case, 'like a lawyer knew about law and other people didn't'. In some cases, he would know more, in others other professionals would make a greater contribution. (H) saw himself as coming into schools sometimes armed with esoteric knowledge, but always with a 'particular viewpoint which may or may not be useful'. Interestingly, this respondent seemed to feel that expectations about expertise and the expert role were often derived from confusing the role styles of psychologists with those of psychiatrists. He still found that members of the public and teachers in school had difficulty in differentiating between the two, and that they construed his contribution as being necessarily akin to that of a medical practitioner.

The fact that many of these respondents felt they could not rely on superior knowledge, in the sense defined above, for all decisions, reinforced the tendency for their role styles to veer towards caution, humility and non-directiveness. In many situations some felt they were merely offering an opinion which teachers could take or leave. Thus (G), who thought deeply about these issues, felt that he had a responsibility for giving an opinion 'at the same time making it clear that the opinion can be rejected'. Others felt that it was an important part of their role merely to talk to teachers as a person rather than a psychologist. Respondent (A), who, as already noted, felt that she spent half her time functioning as an applied scientist, said: 'For the other fifty per cent of my contact with teachers I would just be another person who was in the school'.

Non-directiveness was a very important feature of the role styles of nearly all respondents. It was borne of a belief, that many of them expressed, in the capacities of teachers to work out their own solutions to problems, and in the role of the EP in facilitating this process. This was often linked to an admission that their (i.e., EPs') knowledge of psychology and research findings was of little value or at least of doubtful value in helping teachers to cope with problems. Psychologist (B) provided a lucid account of the dilemmas involved here. To some extent this reflected a contradiction in his approach, because his practice was generally traditionally oriented and he tended to rely on test information as an important resource for decision making. However, he felt that very often it was not a question of providing teachers with information derived from esoteric knowledge, 'great pearls of wisdom', so much as just going into the school and talking at length to the teachers and headteachers so that they could 'reassure themselves that they were doing the best for the kid . . . That seems to take a fair amount of the week really more than actually talking to or seeing individual children'. Even when expertise was appropriate, e.g., in SE procedures, he was doubtful about it. There were so many areas where research findings were contradictory or where research had not been done that it was very difficult to play the expert in relation to any particular problem. He felt that problems were so wide ranging that it was probably impossible for any one psychologist to have sufficient knowledge in depth to claim expertise in most of the areas in which he found himself involved. The difficulty was that teachers often expected him to make such claims — 'I feel a fraud a lot of the time when I'm talking to teachers who regard me as an expert in areas where I don't think I am'. He felt that a good teacher would have most of the knowledge and skills necessary to come up with solutions or at least attempts at solutions which were probably as good as the psychologist's and it was not at all clear whether psychology had any relevance at all. Like teachers, he did not work from psychological theory; he used it occasionally as a resource when he approached problems.

(B) gave the impression of a fairly inexperienced practitioner who was just reaching a stage in his development when some of the contradictions of the job were beginning to surface. He was beginning to look critically at his 'expertise' and its relevance to the problems that were referred to him. Other respondents had perhaps gone through this phase. They had clearly recognized some of the difficulties in 'playing the expert', and had developed a philosophy of practice which enabled them to feel they were making a positive contribution without feeling they needed to preserve an expert image in order to do so. The essence of this philosophy was non-directiveness. (A) felt that one of the main aims of her involvement was to 'get the teacher to decide for herself rather than me doing a diagnosis of the problem'. This did not mean that she did not have her own view of the problem. In fact, in some cases she would probably attempt to steer the teacher towards her perception of the problem, but 'it wasn't as clear cut as this'. In many situations it was important to emphasize a reflective role and accept that the teacher's perception of the problem must be taken into account if she was to be encouraged towards working out a solution 'to what was after all their own problem'. The obvious fact of the matter was that some change was required either of a relatively minor or major nature and she was really there to facilitate this. In the final analysis she would like teachers to solve their own problems and devise their own objectives: 'If formulating objectives was part of the change then I wouldn't like to do it myself but I would like other people to formulate their own objectives'.

Respondent (I) also adopted a non-directive approach in his negotiations with teachers. He considered that he could give the teacher very little information, 'but I can reflect back what the teacher knows already but hasn't articulated in that way or construed in that way . . . and if the teacher doesn't have the information, I can encourage her to get it which I hope is going to be of longer term benefit than my getting and giving the information'. When asked about advising the teacher on objectives in learning to read, he replied: 'There again I would make it reflective . . . I don't have the objectives but then I don't have the problem . . . teachers have an idea of their own objectives . . . If I have objectives they may not be the same ones as the teacher'.

An important consequence of the non-directive approach was that responsibility for change was not taken away from the teacher. Even for respondents who did not adopt as thorough going non-directive approach as (I) this was a key feature. (G) felt 'the helping professions are still seen as people who take away responsibility'. On this point he could make the structure of his practice fairly explicit:

> If I'm involved in a situation which involves children, teacher, school and parents who have primary responsibility and its a responsibility which I can't take away . . . it would be inappropriate. So that defines a lot of what I do. I don't see myself as a direct treatment agent . . . this doesn't relate to the world as it is. I've often run into problems when people's expectations are that I am going to take responsibility and we've got ourselves into great difficulties.

This was not to say that he did not have any responsibilities: 'I think some people in the profession take up a position of no responsibility . . . bouncing back and forth. I think we've a responsibility for giving an opinion at the same time making it clear that the opinion can be rejected.'

Respondent (I) was so concerned that responsibility should not be taken from the teacher that he had to restrain his annoyance when it was clear the teacher had not made much of an effort to sort the problem out for himself — 'It makes me very cross . . . I think well you're being paid for this why aren't you doing anything about it . . . '

The educational context

Most of the respondents were ambivalent about schools. On the one hand they believed in the system sufficiently to want to work within it, but on the other they were critical of certain aspects of schools generally as well as some schools in particular. (B) acknowledged that certain views which he held about primary and secondary schools informed his practice. He did not like what he saw in secondary schools and considered that for children of low ability the present organization was not appropriate for their needs. They really needed a continuation of primary type education. He doubted whether in secondary schools there were coherent sets of objectives for individual pupils. (B) expressed definite views about what he would regard as a 'good school'. It would be one that 'regarded education as being wider than simply the teaching of academic skills . . . I'd think we'd call it a caring school'. It was also a school where there was a 'good' leadership and well-organized pastoral care and disciplinary procedures. (E) was also concerned about the 'caring framework'. His critique of schools was implicit in the way he approached problems. He entered school with his bias towards the child in most instances and set out with the idea that there was nothing wrong with the child and probably something wrong with the school or family. He regarded this as a 'client advocate' approach. His main function was to raise questions about why the child was referred in the first place — an approach which he regarded as 'pretty cynical really'. He expected teachers to tell him what they had already done within a caring framework. (F) felt that schools did not, in the main, achieve the goals which he considered important. He considered it was important for children to learn to read, write and be competent in number, but one of the main aims of education should be 'to teach children to think'. The actual subject matter was not all that important. It was important for children to think rationally and, in terms of transactional analysis, in 'adult' terms, i.e., at the higher levels of Piaget's cognitive model — 'and you certainly *can* teach this because if you went back to look at the number of people who were able to do formal operations at the time of the French Revolution . . . one would imagine that it would be considerably fewer than now'.

Respondent (A) considered that the current education system was far from ideal in terms of criteria that she would consider important. For example, she tended to favour less emphasis on compulsory attendance and more emphasis on allowing children to decide for themselves for how long they wished to continue their studies after a certain age and what they wanted to learn. (G) thought that schools could be improved by feeding in knowledge from psychology. Even very 'basic' psychological knowledge was not in general being used. He believed that an improvement in general relationships would occur:

> if the ratio of positive input to disapproval is 4 to 1 in favour of the former . . . [in schools] this ratio is usually reversed . . . this has been demonstrated fairly clearly . . . if you have an appropriate ratio, you have a generally all round improvement in the behaviour of kids, in teachers feelings about themselves and their job . . . the whole system is affected . . . and this is something that is so trivial.

When asked why the system had failed to take into account this 'trivial' knowledge in the past, he replied:

> I'm a bit unclear on my history here . . . it's something to do with the historical religious background of civilization . . . Calvinism, etc., so you have a whole bias of discipline towards the control of unwanted growth by negative means . . . it's just part of the culture . . . to operate on a disapproval centred basis.

It is clear from these comments that some EPs were conscious of operating in the context of an overall view of the nature of schools and the education system and with some idea of the ideal objectives of education. It should be remembered, of course, that most of the criticisms put forward implied that there was scope for reforming the existing system. There was uncertainty here for some respondents. Thus (A) felt her critique of schools, although it may have influenced her practice in a general way, was to some extent separate from the thoughts that guided here day to day decisions. Although she did not like the system she felt that, given the continuing existence of the system, monitoring standards in basic subjects was a 'good approach'. It is difficult to tell to what extent others adopted this view and split their practice from their beliefs about the system. Certainly some of them became uncertain and vague when it came to expressing their views on the broader social and philosophical aspects of education. Thus (D) felt that 'as soon as you raise questions of change you come to philosophy' and considered himself to be 'a little bit confused', particularly when he considered some of the 'unintended consequences of change'.

CONCLUSION

The overall impression given by these data is that the traditional paradigm is still a considerable force among most practitioners. The questionnaire evidence suggested that most respondents still used intelligence tests on a regular basis, and the analysis of interviews did not reveal a fundamental critique of the basic principles of intelligence testing. Whether or not they used tests regularly or found them relevant to the problems that confronted them daily, most interviewees did not deny that tests were instruments which provided a sample of a child's skills, which was useful for comparing one child with another and for facilitating changes in teacher perception, and that these uses justified the tests' existence. There was concern for the misuse and misinterpretation of test scores by other professionals, but no concern for the possible adverse consequences of relying on such instruments even when they were not misused and not misinterpreted.

It cannot be overemphasized that the questionnaire responses suggested extensive use of individual intelligence tests. The percentage admitting to using the Wechsler Intelligence Scale for Children regularly was not equalled on any other item. These findings do not, therefore, support the view that there has been a huge decline in psychometric testing in Britain, as allegedly there has been in America (see Bersoff, 1973). In fact it is doubtful if the psychometrician is in 'partial eclipse' (see Taylor, 1968) in Britain or America.

It is against this background that the results on the 'perspectives' section must be interpreted. Eclecticism was the most preferred perspective, but it is questionable whether this represented an orientation towards a multiple paradigm approach. The nature of the esoteric knowledge used was conceived mainly as psychological knowledge.

Judging from the emphasis on 'psychology' in other sections of the questionnaire, it seems probable that eclecticism in practice meant feeling free to use ideas from a number of different schools of psychology rather than perspectives which were outside psychology altogether. The impression given was that the traditional paradigm, while not uncritically accepted, was exerting a 'pull' over the range and nature of knowledge that it was considered appropriate for an EP to draw upon in day to day practice.

The 'positivist mentality' also influenced the attitudes towards theory. Among the interviewees a clear distinction was made between 'fact' and 'theory' as if the former were self-evident and independent of the latter, and theories generally were treated in a somewhat 'cavalier' fashion as if unattached to social reality. Thus there were 'facts' about pupils and about teachers which could be stated independently of the social institutions in which they were situated. They did not appear to be aware that the data they relied on to make decisions were full of uncontested presuppositions about the system. For example, most of them considered that it was possible to obtain a profile of 'skills' as if this could be done in a neutral fashion, in a way which did not assume certain educational goals to be desirable.

Clearly other forms of knowledge — philosophical or sociological — could have considerable relevance for these practitioners who were in the business of relating to real life educational problems and had to work with some understanding of the nature of schools as organizations and some awareness of educational issues. But there was no evidence either from the questionnaire or responses from the interviews that respondents were particularly interested in exploring knowledge bases outside psychology which might have illuminated the social and philosophical context of psychological practice.

However, it was clear that many of these practitioners viewed their approach to practice, even if founded on positivist psychology, as a step away from a conventional model. There were at least three aspects that might be interpreted as indicative of a potentially radical change orientation. First, there was clearly some ambivalence shown towards psychometrics. Many respondents and interviewees were clearly developing strategies which did not over-rely on psychometrically derived concepts either at the diagnostic or evaluation stage. There was a move away from norm referenced to criterion referenced and curriculum based approaches. On the questionnaire this was best exemplified by the comments on the use of tests section and by the rank order of lists of perspectives and psychologists which indicated the general popularity of behaviourism, an orientation allegedly with implications for practice considerably different from the psychometric.

Second, all the interviewees claimed to be opposed to the expert role and were consciously trying to break with tradition in this respect. They clearly wanted to adopt a fairly democratic approach in their relations with teachers, and emphasized the role of negotiation. This represented a practitioner philosophy which was clearly opposed to the notion of a helping profession which took upon itself the burden of responsibility for the system's problems. Since medical practitioners have come to be identified as the archetypal helping profession, these interviewees could be described as being opposed to the 'medical model'. Their style was certainly more non-directive than that associated with the stereotype of the medical style.

Third, although there was not a high level of awareness of sociological conceptual frameworks, this was not to say that an appreciation of the significance of educational and social systems *qua* systems was completely absent. As indicated above, many of the interviewees were critical of the way education was organized in schools, and attempted to relate this to a social and historical context. Both questionnaire and interview data suggested an awareness of the importance of 'labelling processess'.

There was some evidence, then, to suggest that many EPs were attempting to develop alternative forms of practice. To what extent these new strategies do represent a genuine break with the traditional paradigm is an open question. In each of the indications of change referred to above there is clearly a theoretical resource involved which, if not new, has not been operationalized in quite the same way before. Both the behavioural orientation and non-directiveness, though rooted in well-known psychological models, seem to imply an approach which leads the practitioner out of the test room or clinic into schools and, when in school, out of the headmaster's study into the classroom. But how radical is this in view of the fact that traditional practitioners have also been concerned about the action taken in schools and classrooms on the basis of their findings? Also, if these 'new' practices still have a psychological knowledge base are they not inevitably limited in situations where clearly what is being aimed at is sustained social change? These and related questions will be discussed in the next two chapters.

CHAPTER 5

The non-directive style

Protagonists of the non-directive approach often explain it in terms of a break with the traditional paradigm. It is first and foremost a style of practice which is anti-expertism. EPs oriented to non-directiveness tend to be those who do not wish to appropriate the responsibilities of teachers or pupils because they feel that given enough freedom and support people develop their own strategies for coping with problems. They are against the idea of a professional group claiming a monopoly of wisdom in relation to psychological problems and maintaining a boundary between themselves and 'lay' people. They consider that the traditional approach to practice is too directive. EPs tried to define the situation in what they thought were realistic terms, but were often only imposing their own constructs on teachers. The non-directive approach implies a more democratic view of the EP-teacher relationship. There is an emphasis on team-work and negotiation.

The non-directive style derives its rationale from a number of different theoretical positions. In the 'sixties and early 'seventies, which is, in the main, the period when this style came to the fore, two of the most popular theories among practitioners were those of George Kelly and Carl Rogers.

On the questionnaire study 18% said they used Kelly regularly and 59% regularly or occasionally. His work has been popularized for EPs by practitioners like Ravenette who have written extensively on applications of personal construct theory to school psychological practice. It is probably true to say that Kelly influenced the appraisal methods of most practitioners, but particularly those who were attempting to formulate an alternative strategy. In a sense, he legitimized the exploratory style that many who were drifting away from psychometrics were already developing, and provided a conceptual framework which did not exclude psychometrics so much as subsume them. Kelly's approach has been described using various labels from which, in the main, he has disassociated himself. But it seems reasonable to suggest that important influences include cognitive psychology, phenomenology and self theories of personality. It is not as explicitly anti-expert as the Rogerian model, but has the same democratic 'climate' surrounding it in application, and it certainly implies an appreciative and non-directive style which focuses on the person's subjectivity as the starting point of an investigation. It has more to say about appraisal methods than the Rogerian model which is better known for its application to 'treatment', although no sharp division between 'diagnosis' and 'therapy' can be made in relation to either of these models.

The Rogerian approach was reasonably popular among EPs in the survey, with 15% claiming to use Rogers regularly and 66% either regularly or occasionally; 10% claimed to strongly prefer a humanistic perspective and 9% a phenomenological. Virtually none of those who favoured Rogerian, humanistic or phenomenological approaches were exclusively oriented in the direction suggested by these descriptions. Most combined one or more of these with eclecticism, developmental or even a behaviourist perspective. Nevertheless it is worth noting the popularity of these perspectives, because Rogers, in particular, has been linked with radical practice and his relative popularity may represent a chink in the armour of the traditional paradigm.

One of the interviewees in the previous chapter who considered he had made a significant break with tradition acknowledged the influence of Rogers and Kelly. It is instructive to look at the views of this respondent, (I), in more detail.

As noted previously, he considered psychometrics to be virtually irrelevant to the kinds of question he wanted to ask. Having received a referral, he immediately threw the problem back to the teacher: 'Perhaps the child is not doing what the teacher wants him to do . . . it's important that he gets the people involved to look at that and decide what they think.' He felt there was little information that he could give the teacher which was useful, but considered that his role was to reflect back what the teacher knew already but had not articulated. Likewise, he was reflective when talking about teaching objectives. The fact that his own values often 'came through' made him all the more determined not to put his values across. He was fairly accepting of most schools of psychology but tended to be rather negative about psychoanalysis because of its association with medicine and psychiatry. He felt he would always tend to favour the non-directive approach because 'I want people to determine their own futures . . . to decide what they want to do. I am willing to help them sort it out for themselves . . . but I don't want to impose my outlook on them.' He considered himself to be person centred, but admitted there were lots of contradictions in this approach. Children were compelled to go to school between five and sixteen years of age and he had to work within this system and yet this was not always compatible with their best interests. 'I would want each child to develop personally as fully as possible and in some cases I would see that as happening more easily outside the formal school situation. I would want each teacher to do the same.'

He was not sure about a programme for change, but he thought a good starting point would be that there should be a little less compulsion than there was now — 'see how that worked and then try even less compulsion'. He thought there were plenty of obvious ways that schools did not meet a child's natural or 'artificial' needs.

There are two aspects in this account which appear to represent a radical break with the traditional model. First, there is the desire not to impose his own constructs on the teachers and the respect for and recognition of teacher and pupil autonomy. This, as we shall see, is clearly a perspective which can be derived from both Rogers and Kelly. Second, there is an educational orientation which appears to be based on a broad conception of human potential and a critical approach to the current situation in schools. The importance of the school context as an arena for change is also typical of the two theories under discussion.

But to what extent does the approach to practice derived from these theories represent a genuine alternative to the traditional paradigm? The following analysis of both theories in action addresses itself to this question.

PERSONAL CONSTRUCTS

An approach to practice based on Kelly's model would be more concerned with diagnosis and with the cognitive rather than effective aspects of functioning, but would share the Rogerian's concern for the importance of understanding a person's subjectivity — the inner world of private, personal meanings — and the need to avoid imposing one's own constructs on the client. Kelly's starting point for psychological theorizing is a model of man which he calls 'man-the-scientist' — a model which contrasts with the biological reductionist and determinist models of the traditional paradigm.

'Let us then instead of occupying ourselves with man-the-biological-organism, or man-the-lucky-guy have a look at man-the-scientist' (1955, p4). Man is a scientist because his main concern is with prediction and control which is achieved through developing personal constructs. Such constructs are personal interpretations which enable him to anticipate and thus control events in his milieu. They are called 'personal constructs' as opposed to 'categories' or 'concepts' partly in order to underline the fact that they have been invented by an active, creative individual and partly because they have special properties which distinguish them from these other terms. A personal construct although it shares the bipolarity of traditional categories has an additional property of contrast and can only be fully understood in terms of a contrastive pole. These contrastive poles are often 'submerged' but we need to understand them before the meaning of a construct can be clarified. The contrastive pole is not the logical opposite of the construct (e.g., table/not table; kindness/unkindness) but the contrast which is peculiar to the individual concerned, so that for one person the submerged pole of 'kindness' might be 'cruelty' for another it might be 'indifference'.

Constructs are always interpretations of situations rather than situations themselves, but are necessary for anticipating or predicting events in the real world. These events can provide evidence which either supports or does not support predictions based on constructs. No two people will construe events in exactly the same way. Constructs are interrelated in hierarchical systems, i.e., superordinate and subordinate constructs, and the 'core constructs' are extremely important for maintaining a person's identity. Sometimes constucts are tightly organized leading to rigid thinking, sometimes they are loose enabling the person to think more flexibly and creatively. Construct systems have 'ranges of convenience' — all the things or events for which the user finds each system useful; and 'focuses of convenience' — those matters for which the system is maximally useful. Elements are the persons, things or events abstracted by the construct and any one of these can provide the construct with its name.

If a person's prediction is not 'validated', he may either change the construct or turn to other constructs in his repertoire. Constructs and thus predictions can be changed in the light of experience and new constructs formed. Certain conditions are notoriously unfavourable for the development of new constructs. When a person feels threatened — that is, when there is an awareness of an imminent major change in his core constructs — he is unlikely to be flexible enough to explore alternative constructs. Several other forms of 'deviant' conduct can be defined in terms of personal constructs. Guilt is the awareness of the separation of the self from one's core role constructs. Anxiety is the awareness that one's constructs are inadequate to deal with the task at hand. Hostility is the continued effort to validate a prediction shown to be a failure.

A person's construct system may be changed by deliberate intervention, e.g., psychotherapy, or as part of the 'natural' course of events as a person moves from one context to another. Thus, there may be a shift in the construct system when a person moves from town into the country or moves from one occupation to another. A key aspect of a person's ability to adjust to new circumstances is whether or not his constructs are of a kind that will enable flexible thinking. This will depend on the permeability of his constructs, i.e., the capacity for a construct to be used as a referent for a novel event. Pre-emptive constructs are those which regard people or events as 'real things' which can only be named by a particular construct. If a child is of low intelligence then he is nothing but of low intelligence. Propositional constructs are more exploratory and hypothesis generating. To look at a child as of low intelligence is only one way of looking at him; there are many others, and low intelligence may not be a particularly useful one and could, depending on how we choose, be dropped at any time.

Kelly's model of a 'social relationship' refers to those instances where social actors understand each others' 'systems of constructs'. The sociality corollary states that 'to the extent that one person construes the construction processes of another, he may play a role in a social process involving the other person'. Understanding the world of personal meaning of another person enables us to relate to that other person and predict their behaviour. If we do not understand their constructs, our interpretations will be rather hit and miss and of poor predictive power.

The philosophical position at the root of Kelly's model is constructive alternativism. No one needs to be hemmed in by circumstances or be victims of their own biography. The events we face are open to as many interpretations as our wits are able to contrive. The way we perceive the world is continually open to question and the most mundane occurrences of everyday life can be transformed if we are creative enough to construe them differently. The only limits on this process are imposed by our 'feeble wits'. We are always in a position of uncertainty because we are always aware that others' interpretations may be even more valid than ours.

The investigation of subjectivity

Practising psychologists have never been adverse to exploring mind and consciousness but there has been a tendency for those working within the traditional paradigm to treat the 'hard' data of psychometrics as superior to the 'soft' data obtained from investigating subjectivity. During the late 'sixties and early 'seventies, however, a method came to the fore which seemed to have all the advantages of a subjectivist approach without denying the importance of the positivist's concern with rigour and quantification. This was known as the Repertory Grid Technique which involved similar psychological processes to the old 'projective' tests but derived from a Kellyian rather than psychoanalytic model.

In the Grid Technique described by Kelly (1955, p. 242) the subject supplies the names of various role titles — self, father, mother, sister, etc. — which are written on cards and laid out before the subject who is asked to suggest an important way in which two of the people are alike and different from the third. He may for example indicate that father and mother are both 'sad' whereas sister is 'happy'. This is the first construct to be elicited and the tester records this on the Grid Form — squared paper with horizontal columns representing the role titles and the vertical representing constructs. The tester puts ticks in the appropriate grid cells for father and mother and leaves the cell for sister blank. He then asks the subject to look at other people named on the cards and indicate which of them he would also call 'sad' rather than 'happy'. The tester ticks the cells or leaves them blank according to the subject's response. The same process is repeated for another three role titles and so on until several constructs have been elicited. These are allegedly constructs from the repertoire (thus the term repertory grid) which the subject uses to structure his inner world. Once the grid has been filled in we are in a position to analyse the relationships between the constructs as they function in his system. Some constructs may match highly or may be virtually equivalent, others may have a negative relationship. It is not difficult to see how the degree of association between constructs can be calculated using statistics and also how the results might be subjected to factor analysis.

This is the original Role Construct Repertory Grid Technique, and there have been many variations on it. For example, rather than use role titles we could use the names of peers, photographs, objects, situations, or any other list of 'elements' that was considered appropriate. Or the elements could be ranked on each construct and the rankings listed to provide a matrix which could be treated statistically in various ways.

How adequate is this method for investigating a person's subjectivity? We should remember that what we are trying to find out is not the person's standing on a dimension or ranking on a construct that we have provided but the nature of that person's 'cognitive map', his structured constellation of personal meanings, reflecting the very core of his identity as well as the more peripheral areas. After all, a person is his personal constructs. Bearing this in mind the Grid Techinque clearly has certain limitations.

To begin with an assumption is made about the relevance of the elements to a person's world. It may be that the elements the tester chooses represent aspects of a person's world which are only marginal or which have no relevance at all to his core constructs. For example, it cannot even be guaranteed that members of the immediate family are significant in this respect. The person may relate most strongly to people not indicated in the role list which Kelly employed. Thus elements have to be elicited as well as constructs, but this presupposes a great deal of interpretative work on the part of both tester and testee before the Grids are introduced. This, of course, would include working out which universe of elements would be most appropriate. In short, we already have to have a considerable understanding of a person's subjectivity before the technique can be employed.

Second, an assumption is made that the word label used by the person means roughly the same to him as it does to the tester. This perhaps is not so important on the Grid as it is, say, in the more traditional instruments like personality tests and questionnaires, because whatever the labels a good deal of information can be obtained from an analysis of the relationship between them. However, the problem is not completely resolved in this way, and the tester really needs to have additional information on the testee's use of language.

A third assumption is related to the use of Grids in a way which blatantly violates some of the most important principles of the theory. In practice, the constructs are often provided rather than elicited, and the tester proposes to the client the elements to be sorted. Assumptions are being made here about the representativeness of the constructs and the sorts. This is usually done for sound, practical reasons but too often the significance of the 'violation' for interpreting the data goes unrecognized.

But perhaps the most crucial limitation of the technique is one that, in fact, does not result from violating the theory but from faithfully applying the notion of construct. Triadic elicitation is an appropriate method if one accepts the nature of a personal construct as one that can only be understood in terms of its contrastive pole. But is this an adequate description of the way people think? As Taylor (1976) argues a contrastive pole might enable the meaning of a construct to be refined, but it is not the only way that meaning can be attributed to a construct. It is important to understand the context in which the construct is being used. Sometimes a contrastive pole can highlight certain features of the construct which are relevant in a particular context.

> The complex nature of categories, consisting as they do of a large number of defining attributes, means they have a wide latitude of interpretation, but when a category is used in a particular context certain of its attributes become more salient than others, though all are necessary to define it. Thus in one situation it may be those attributes which distinguish bus from lorry which are important (for vehicle excise duty for example) while in another context it may be those attributes which mark it off from a train which are most significant. (Taylor p. 185)

It is in this way that one can conceive of the contrastive pole as a useful but not the only way of providing 'additional contextual support'. It cannot, however, of itself define the construct because 'at some point along the line positive attributes are required to give meaning to the construct' e.g., a bus is a unique combination of attributes — it is a vehicle, it has an engine and a driver, it carries passengers, etc.

Taylor's point is, quite simply, that people do not only think in the way Kelly thinks they do but in other ways as well. It is therefore scarcely surprising that, with their habitual mode of thinking being geared in another direction, people may perceive sorting triads as just an artificial and contrived a task as any invented by psychometricians.

In summary, then, this theory and technique do not seem to represent such a radical break with the traditional approach. At the theoretical level we have a conception of people's constructs which seems to be based on an unnecessarily restricted view of how they think, and probably one which is not much of an improvement on the psychometrician's assumptions about what constitutes intelligence. But even if the theory itself has more good points than bad, in its application to practice in the form of the Repertory Grid Technique, many of the hallmarks of the 'positivist mentality' are evident: the rush into quantification, the lack of respect for theory and, in the final analysis, the unacknowledged imposition of one's own assumptions.

Many of the best examples of Kelly's model in action are, in fact, those where no attempt is made to treat constructs in a statistical way. In these cases, the approach is much more exploratory and dialectical.

Exploration in a social context

Ravenette provides many example of how the general application of personal construct theory can illuminate some of the typical 'problems' with which EPs are faced: reading difficulties, 'low' intelligence and maladjustment. The theory is employed to provide a perspective which results in a different appraisal emphasis from the traditional approach. Instead of the child being treated as an object, he is seen 'as a subject, in his own right', and knowledge of how he construes himself in relation to the learning process is considered crucial to a full understanding of the problem. Thus, when investigating a reading problem, Ravenette (1968) recommends that we follow Kelly and 'find out if the child likes the teacher' as well as 'if the teacher, or parent likes the child, and at the same time is not forcing the child into a role which is inappropriate and is not depriving the child of the means of developing his own identity in a constructive way, not using the child to meet his own needs.' (page 76-77) The same author is critical of much of the research done on intelligence because it has been done at too simple a level, and has emphasized mathematical and statistical aspects at the expense of operating at a level involving understanding children and how their capacities develop. He proposes a more sophisticated model which takes into account several approaches to intelligence, the first of which is based on the assumption that the child is seen 'as an essentially active being who progressively constructs a sense of order out of his experiences with the world and is able to operate effectively within it'. (Ravenette 1974, p. 16). This, of course, is the view of the child at root of a genre of psychological theories from cognitive to humanistic and contrasts with that of the child as an 'information processing' organism. We are also indebted to Ravenette for some of the most sensitive and insightful descriptions of Kelly's model applied to the exploration of maladjustment from the teacher's viewpoint. One example will suffice:-

The non-directive style / 95

> When a teacher describes a child to us and gives an account of his behaviour she is giving us at the same time an example of her own personal map for making sense of children. It is not always easy for a teacher to select from what she knows the things she thinks we want to know... We can ask her to give three adjectives which she feels best describe this boy. These will be a selection from her constructs. We can then ask her to document each construct with more observations. The teacher says that Lewis is a 'loving' boy, he will put an arm round you affectionately. He is forgiving after he has been punished. If we pursue the opposite of loving i.e. 'hating' which seems to be the equivalent of her second adjective 'aggressive', she adds that he is often cruel to little girls or anyone smaller... He does not hate adults whom he respects. His foster father beats him. 'Loving' also leads her to an elaboration of 'generous' which the teacher had used at the outset. He is generous all the time, with children and with adults... Her third adjective was 'willing'. He will notice if you want something before you ask for it and get it... We can... go further by asking the teacher to relate three ways she has been surprised by [the boy in question], etc. (1972, p44).

There is a world of difference between this style and the one which is encouraged by formally administering a Rep Grid. We can see how the approach here might be called 'naturalistic' in that the process of appraisal seems to sit more easily in the natural flow of conversation about a child between teacher and psychologist. Inherent in this process are ample checks against either party being diverted into irrelevant areas, or becoming involved in activities which are transparently artificial or trivial. The psychologist is adopting a genuinely exploratory approach and is appreciative of the teacher's position, e.g., 'It is not easy for a teacher...' There is no required procedure to follow ('If we pursue...') and everything is a matter of choice and decisions taken on a moment to moment basis according to the 'signposts' in the conversation.

Kelly's theory applied to practice certainly places interaction with others at the centre of professional activity. It is impossible to construe the construction processes of another unless we ask them about their constructs and this entails communication and a fairly deep level of involvement. A criticism of the positivist expert was that it was too easy for him to 'hide behind tests' or deliver interpretations based on what amounted to a superficial overview of the problem.

However, there is an important sense in which Kelly's theory is not social enough. Although he recognizes that the teacher is located in an interpersonal world, the constraining features of the school context are not given their full weight. These constraints to some extent influence the way the teacher construes or is able to construe the 'world of the classroom'. Constructs, in fact, are more correctly regarded as 'typifications' rather than personal categories; that is, as part of what Berger and Luckman (1967, p. 45) regard as 'typificatory schemes in terms of which others are apprehended and "dealt with" in face to face encounters'. These typifications may have been 'negotiated' over the years and have been 'handed down' to the teachers via the culture in which they are located. They emanate from social givens which existed prior to the teacher's 'entrance' into the education system. They are not solely a product of teacher's personal 'devising', but 'run deep' in the system, within the culture and organization of the school and the interactive contex, and are influenced by the nature and distribution of material resources and the wider structural context. For example, a construct like 'intelligent' may be creatively employed by the teacher in relation to a particular pupil and may have a place in the teacher's system of personal constructs, but it is also an idea with a history which has helped to establish the current organizational structure and cultural climate of the school. It has a certain affinity to the teacher's interest, e.g., how to explain away the slow progress of certain groups of children, and is made available to teachers via their socialization and training. This underplaying of social constraints leads to a model of change which has certain strengths, but which, in the final analysis, is too simplistic. If changes are considered necessary it is not sufficient to assume that they will occur and be maintained merely if one or two individual teachers reconstruct their construct systems. Such reconstruction is important, but what is just as important is the recognition of the institutional framework also as an object of change. This obvious fact is often forgotten by those who plump for attitude changes as the key element in a programme of reform or remediation, and then find that what ultimately happens is that the 'new' vocabulary supposedly reflecting the changed attitude becomes a rhetoric — the original meanings are distorted and the same circumstances occur under a different name.

In Kelly's theory the individual is conceived in a more social way but processes are analysed in terms of individual consciousness and individual meeting individual, with no other level being considered. However, the fact that the individual is considered as an active agent rather than a passive object, and that the subjectivity of the person is taken seriously represents a significant shift of emphasis from the traditional approach.

THE SELF ACTUALIZING TENDENCY

According to Rogers 'the organism has one basic tendency and striving — to actualise, maintain and enhance the experiencing organism' (Rogers, 1951, p. 487). If the individual is to avoid psychological tension and thus unhealthy development, his awareness of self must be congruent with organismic experiences. In his more recent works Rogers has used the word 'realness' rather than 'congruence'. 'Realness' is about being in touch with feelings. Feelings are for Rogers virtually reducible to psychological tensions and are experienced prior to cognitive awareness. Coming to terms with the real feeling self is an important and, for the future of mankind, essential task for everyone.

There are several problems with this approach. One might agree with Rogers that being out of touch with feelings is not a 'good thing' and that it is not healthy to bottle up feelings or to 'sit on' emotions. However, one would worry about where Rogers' particular formulation of these issues might lead. For example, it is one thing to recognize 'feelings' as an underdeveloped part of human potential, it is quite another to consider them to be primary experience and to stem from the reactions of an organism. There is a tendency for a Rogerian to assume that because feelings are primary and genuine they must be accepted. Indeed, if we are being honest, we do not have much choice other than to accept them because we are not fully in control of them. Feelings are crucial, but they just happen often in uncontrolled fashion because they arise from the reactions of the human organism.

Against this one could argue that feelings do not spring directly into consciousness as a result of biological necessity. They are socially mediated and, although 'natural' in one sense, are no more so than our desire to deny, repress or discriminate between them. There might be a case for referring to unneccessary repression of emotions in relation to some particular activity. Thus not to recognize angry feelings in personal relationships does not ultimately make for good marriages and friendships in our society. But this is not to say that all emotions and feelings in all situations must always be accepted. Rather than always accepted feelings, as Rogers suggests, it is possible to imagine situations for the 'good' of ourselves and others when it is appropriate to purge certain feelings which restrict growth rather than enhance it.

An overemphasis on feelings can have consequences which are just as restricting as an overemphasis on the cognitive and intellectual. It might lead to something akin to the 'awareness craze' so vividly described and analysed by Schur:

> Every emotion has value, according to the new ideology. We must recognise all feelings, express them, open them up to the people around us. We must in short let it all hang out. If we accept this view there seems little room for us to discriminate among our emotions or control our feelings. (1976, p. 17)

The language of the 'awareness craze' pervades the stated aims and objectives of those who advocate 'psychological education' as part of the normal school curriculum. Hopson and Hough (1976), who refer to mental health statistics to justify the need for a systematic approach to the personal and social education of young people in secondary schools, describe a model for personal growth which includes objectives like awareness of relationships between physical and emotional expression, awareness of emotion in self and others, learning to accept all feelings as valid, effective expression of feelings, etc.

There is nothing objectionable about these goals *per se*. That they should be regarded as only part of personal growth is duly recognized by Hopson and Hough. They include 'thinking' and 'doing' objectives as well as 'sensing' and 'feeling'. However, Schur's critique should certainly be taken seriously, for there is evidence that despite an overt concern with intellect and concious social change, many of the 'awareness' groups in America have encouraged a drift into self-absorption, anti-intellectualism and mysticism. Psychological practice which is based on a theory like that of Rogers could easily lead to an approach to personal growth which is inward-looking and overemphasizes the 'feeling' side.

The non-directive role

Reflecting the feeling tones is essentially what the psychologist is up to in client-centred therapy. In *Counselling and Psychotherapy* (1942) Rogers mentions four features as distinguishing characteristics of what he describes as the 'newer approach' to therapy. First, there is an aim at greater independence of the individual with freedom for spontaneous growth on his part. Second, more stress is laid on the affective as opposed to the intellectual elements. Third, there is a greater stress on the immediate situation than on past events. Fourth, the therapeutic relationship is seen as a growth experience in itself. The non-directive psychologist views the client as being capable of dealing constructively with his own problems and sees the responsibility for reorganizing himself to lie with the client. This does not mean that the psychologist adopts a passive role. Passivity can be experienced as rejection and is inconsistent with the Rogerian value of regarding the client as a person of worth. The psychologist does not really experience the hates, hopes and fears of his client but perceives them through sinking himself in an empathetic process. 'To sense the client's inner world or private personal meanings as if it were your own, but without ever having the "as if" quality, this is empathy . . .' (Rogers, 1965, p. 95).

There is virtually no role for diagnosis in the Rogerian approach. The diagnostic role, in fact, places one in an unhelpful, superior position to the client. Even if one does attain knowledge of causes in the diagnostic interview, it is very unlikely that one would actually make use of this 'cold' information. In *Client-Centred Therapy* Rogers refers to diagnostic procedures as not only unnecessary but also detrimental. The locus of evaluation should not be in the expert. Ultimately, according to Rogers, diagnosis implies acceptance of a society where there is social control of the many by the few. The psychologist's job is to empathize, to reflect the feeling tone, to establish a therapeutic climate which is warm, accepting and genuine; not to clarify, interpret and evaluate. The ultimate test of whether or not one believes in the capacity of the client to solve his own problems is if one is completely willing for any outcome to be chosen. Even when death is contemplated the therapist still continues to reflect the feeling tones because 'it is as he is willing for death to be the choice that life is chosen' (1951, p. 49).

Although this approach may provide a necessary counter-force to the excesses of the directive school, it cannot be said to have removed all directive elements. Even the most non-directive of psychologists has to come to terms with the fact that some form of ongoing assessment and interpretation on his part is inevitable. Assessment is clearly part of what is involved in all interpersonal relationships. Heritage (1974) points out that 'assessing people is an integral and vital part of social interaction' which 'gears in with the practical purposes of everyday life' (p. 274). If there is no mutual assessment, there may be no relationship. Likewise, if empathy involves perception of feelings and perception involves interpretation, if there is no interpretation there may be no empathy. The reflection of feeling tones merely implies that the psychologist reflects his interpretation of the feeling tones. It follows that the psychologist is still in a position to control and manipulate, but in a way which is less obvious than in directive counselling. Green (1946) sees client centred therapy as 'simply a subtle way of getting across to the client the cues which indicate approval of cultural values'. Clients have difficulty in 'kicking' against the non-directive psychologist because there is nothing obvious to direct criticism at. Here is a person who presents himself as equal, democratic and accepting. Yet, ultimately, the client construes himself in line with the psychologist's perspective. As in all successful counselling, the client arrives at a position where his self definition is in the 'style' and language of the particular school of psychology to which the psychologist belongs. One of Rogers' clients remarks: 'I haven't finished the job of integrating and reorganising myself, but that's only confirming, not discouraging, now that I realise this is a continuing process' (1951, p. 88).

In the light of this discussion, it seems unlikely that humanistically-oriented EPs could completely avoid being directive. However hard they tried to be 'neutral' like Respondent (I), it would be difficult not to allow their own values and opinions to interfere with the 'natural growth' processes of their clients, teachers or pupils. Inevitably, the EPs' own conceptual frameworks would influence the course of negotiation with teachers and the practices that emerged would only be radically oriented if the ideas that dominated the negotiations were radical ones. There appears to be nothing radical about the reflective role *per se*. The most one can say is that by being non-directive in his general approach to teachers the EP has at least to put himself in a position of listening attentively to what the teacher has to say about the problem or any other matter that springs to mind which may or may not be related to the problem. In this way, the EP has a chance to understand the teacher's situation more fully. Although it is not the only way to become appreciative of the teacher perspective, it may offer more scope than a directive approach.

Self-directed change in schools

As indicated above, the non-directive approach implies that change must be self directed. But there is nowhere in Rogers' work or in that of any other advocate of the non-directive approach a satisfactory illustration of a change process which can claim to be genuinely self directed. For example, in *Freedom to Learn* (1969) where Rogers fleshes out his outline plan for what he describes as self-directed change, most of the important initiatives do not come from individuals working in schools, but from the 'facilitator' in a target educational institution selected because one or two powerful administrators have expressed a willingness to participate in an encounter group.

The facilitator is the key figure. Although there is a concern that as many people as possible should become facilitators, certainly in the initial stages of change the facilitator would be the 'expert', though he may choose not to regard himself as such. The facilitator is more than just an 'aware', 'real' person, for he is not only competent in those personal and interpersonal skills required for successfully establishing the appropriate social climate for an encounter group but he is 'cognitively' developed and grounded in the behavioural sciences.

The non-directive educational psychologist is caught in a similar position. Whether he likes it or not his immersion in psychology is inevitably reflected in the nature of his influence on teachers. The knowledge that certain processes, such as the self-actualizing tendency, becoming 'real' etc., are of crucial importance leads to a subtle shift of emphasis towards support for practitioner definitions which recognize and highlight these particular features. Many people's experience of encounter groups, for example, is that their own preoccupations are only considered relevant if they can be described in language approved by the facilitator. A problem for the facilitator is that although he would like to be reflective, his knowledge of psychology 'intrudes' on his reflections. He finds it difficult not to conceive of this knowledge as expertise because ultimately it is grounded in a positivist view of psychology.

In Rogerian theory and practice there is a central paradox which is never resolved. On the one hand there is concern for ego development, self awareness, the realization of potential so that individuals will have enough confidence, maturity and self knowledge to make rational choices in the light of their own needs and wants and to take control of their own lives. And yet, on the other hand, it is evident that the range of choice is limited and that forces outside the individual play an important determining role. What is not generally accepted, or at least is certainly underplayed, is that for some individuals the choice is more limited than for others and that for many choice may be totally sacrificed to the needs of society. At school choices are not only limited by what is available but also by the image of abilities and personality which the school provides for the individual. As Henry (1966) points out: 'School metamorphoses the child, giving it the kind of self the school can manage and then proceeds to minister to the self it has made.'

The heady optimism exuded by Rogerians about individualistic approaches to change is typical of most humanistic psycholgists. They feel that their psychology injected into schools would counter the depersonalization and dehumanization which are typical features of these establishments. Even a dash of humanistic psychology may do wonders for the drab, impersonal social climate of schools. Pupils and teachers could usefully spend more time focusing on problems of a personal and interpersonal kind. Patterson (1974) asserts that 'the only solution to our social problems' is the production of self actualized persons, not more scientists, engineers and technicians who can 'relatively easily solve the technical aspects of our problems of poverty, pollution and population' (p. 7). It is the psychological aspects which have proved the most intractable.

This is heady stuff. But are social problems to be tackled in this way? Hazell (1973) provides a good illustration of how individualistic models of change may produce naive practices in the face of certain prevailing social and political realities. He describes depersonalization as a pervasive problem in higher education and recommends that moves should be made towards the creation of a growth environment. This entails making students feel safe and secure. As Guntrip (1968) suggests, the way to do this is to make the students feel 'real' by imparting to them an 'experience of relationship'. Overt friendliness and concentration upon problems and their interpretation are of secondary importance. What is more important is to sense one's own reality and this can only be achieved within a relationship whose main quality is one of being rather than doing.

The solution advocated is for counsellors to be employed who can 'reach' students. However, there is no attempt to come to terms with features of the wider society which provide the overall ideological and structural underpinnings of depersonalization in higher education. In particular, there are the 'competitive' aspects of society. Hazell himself admits that 'we need to resolve a strong tendency *in a competitive society* to equate tenderness with a weakness which is felt to be intolerable'. Higher education is imbued with a competitive ideology which it also helped to create. Hazell himself clearly attributes some causal weight to the prevailing 'competitiveness'. Yet his solution appears to do little to alter these circumstances. If he has a broader perspective on change, there is certainly no indication as to how the wide-ranging changes required for an assault on 'competitiveness' in society at large follow from his recomendations.

Rogerian theory appeals because it seems to offer a rationale for solving problems in a relatively easy fashion. It is a 'here and now' psychology which makes individuals feel optimistic that they can make a contribution. All that is required is for individuals to focus on their particular interpersonal world and to improve their own relating, communicating and 'realness' and thus grow towards self actualization. It means that everyone can feel like an active agent making a vital contribution to his own and other people's destinies.

But there is a catch. For the individual, the preoccupation with the problematics derived from this theory is a never-ending preoccupation. Aiming for autonomy, individuality and personal growth in our society is very much like chasing shadows. Identity crises are forever recurring and are not just a problem of youth. People are encouraged to be in touch with a 'real self' which is not fixed but everchanging. As life develops, old 'real' selves are cast aside and new ones take their place. It is no wonder we experience this as 'crisis' if we think the real self is our natural self. Something basic and fundamental seems to be in constant shift and therefore requires our constant attention and interest. The self actualized person we aim to be is not transfixed in this way. He is in fact just the opposite. As Maslow (1956) points out: 'He is not ego-centred, but focuses on problems outside himself, even being mission oriented.' But essentially he is a superman, an ideal, rather than actually attainable by the majority in our society. The lot of most people who accept the humanistic message is the endless toil of Sisyphus.

For Jacoby (1975) self theory appeals as a last resort of desperate men in search of subjectivity. 'The ego — or self, individuality, subjectivity — moves to the fore in psychological thought just as in fact it is preparing to exit from existence' (p. 47). This is the main thrust of his poignant critique of humanistic psychology which he elaborates in the context of a comparison with what he regards as the far more revolutionary theory of Freud. For him, humanistic and self psychology is conformist psychology. It emphasizes immediacy and the 'here and now' and ignores the history of the wider social reality in which interpersonal relationships are embedded. That wider social reality contains increasingly monolithic and all-embracing exploitative forces which signal the demise of the human subject.

However, there is no doubt that 'change' is at the heart of the Rogerian definition of social reality.

> The world is changing at an exponential rate. If our society is to meet the challenge of the dizzying changes in science, technology,

104 / The Cautious Expert

> communication and social relationships, we cannot rest on the answers provided in the past, but must put our trust in the *processes* by which new problems are met. (1969, p. 313)

For Rogers, the changing world is something that is happening outside the individual to which the individual responds, but it is not clear what role there is for the individual in actually creating this changing world. Knowledge and skills become obsolete; new skills and new knowledge emerge, again to become obsolete. If the individual is to cope with this flux he must not concentrate on questions and answers but rather on 'processes'. Where do autonomy, independence and choice come into this model? Only processes are to be focused on and this seems to preclude a discussion as to whether or not the 'dizzying changes' are necessary or desirable in the first place. Why is this skill needed? Why does this job have to be done? Why does this object have to be produced? A process model refers to healthy ways of adapting to changes, but the 'changing world' seems to be the driving force pulling personality and self along in its wake. Flexibility, openness, adaptability, responsivness are desirable traits because they enable the individual to accommodate to the 'changing world' rather than take control of it. Adaptation to existing circumstances rather than control of one's own destiny seems, in the final analysis, to be the message of Rogerian psychology.

CONCLUSION

In this chapter I have attempted to demonstrate that the theories of neither Kelly nor Rogers provided as radical a break from the traditional paradigm as many practitioners of the late 'sixties and early 'seventies hoped they would. Both are founded on assumptions about man which are individualist and, in the case of Rogers, have a biological reductionist flavour. In practice, if not necessarily in theory, both lead to distinctly partial views of psychological processes. A Rogerian perspective overemphasizes feeling at the expense of cognition and the historical content of experience. Kelly's constructs with their contrastive poles represent a rather limited and fragmented view of the way people think and use language. I have tried to show that the concept of self-directed change is confused in the way that Rogers uses it to describe a plan for change in the education system, and how Kelly's model of change is based on a view of man in society which is not social enough. I have also tried to demonstrate the directiveness of the non-directive approach and show how the values of the Rogerian therapist come through, and how the tendency for the constructs of a Kellyian examiner to be imposed on the examinee results from the influence of the 'positivist mentality' on the appraisal process.

It is interesting that both these psychologists have more in common with the 'dynamic' rather than the 'static' aspects of 'modern educational psychology' referred to in Chapter 1. In this sense they may be said to hark back to a previous period when psychology was more closely tied in with the progressive movement in education. Although they would have opposed her psychoanalytic views, it is probably true that both have more in common with a psychologist like Susan Isaacs than one like Cyril Burt. Yet, like the 'dynamic' psychologists of old, an EP using the non-directive style is still operating within what I have described as the traditional paradigm, rather than in a way that represents a genuine alternative.

CHAPTER 6

The behavioural approach

Behavioural psychology has long been a dominant influence in American psychology and relatively recent reviews indicate that the trend is still in this direction (Burns and Rupiper, 1977). In Britain, there is also evidence that behavioural psychology is becoming increasingly popular. In the AEP journal there has been an increase in the number of articles on behaviour modification in recent years. In the survey carried out by the author behaviourism was a popular orientation among EPs. It was third ranked in a list of perspectives and 76% of respondents either strongly or weakly preferred it. Skinner was the most regularly used psychologist, and Tansley, who is primarily concerned with a behavioural 'skills' approach to the analysis of learning difficulties, was the most drawn upon educationist. One of the most popular books was the behaviourally oriented *Learning and Behaviour Difficulties in School* by Leach and Raybould (1977). In a career information sheet, the AEP in describing the role of the EP referred specifically to behaviour modification techniques, but not to any other treatment orientation, apart from 'counselling' which, of course, can also be behavioural (see Woody, 1968).

The application of behavioural psychology to education was largely a development of the 'seventies. Programmed learning and behaviour therapy had long been part of the psychologists' repertoire, but it was not until the early 'seventies that EPs in Britain began referring to behaviour modification techniques in relation to the treatment of 'maladjusted' children and children with 'learning difficulties'. This renewed interest in behaviourally oriented practice coincided with the reaction against the informal, progressive ideology which dominated the 'sixties. The first article in the *Journal* of the Association of Educational Psychologists referring to the 'new' approach appeared in 1972 (see Presland). Although this article purports to be concerned with 'maladjusted behaviour generally', it is not without significance that the emphasis, judging from the examples provided, is on behaviours considered to be 'disruptive' or 'management problems'.

THE BEHAVIOURAL APPROACH

Although this approach is founded in behaviouristic psychology, it is more eclectic than this description implies. In practice the behaviourist assumptions are supplemented by other psychological principles. Presland (1976), for example, a leading advocate of the behavioural approach considered that 'behaviour modification' was 'now really a rather misleading term'. Although he recommended that programmes of remediation should seek their rationale in Skinner's model, in fact it was possible to synthesize this with apparently contradictory models which, for example, assumed that learning should be considered 'meaningful'. Strictly speaking, therefore, we are not talking about 'crude' behaviourism so much as a behaviourally-oriented or more simply a behavioural approach. This approach has been used in curriculum-based assessment and remediation programmes for children with learning difficulties and in the development of behaviour modification programmes for 'problem' behaviour.

Curriculum based assessment and evaluation

Ainscow and Tweddle (1977) have suggested that EPs would find the approach useful in their 'dealings with remedial departments in normal schools and individual children'. They describe how complex skills such as reading and handwriting can be broken down into sequences of behavioural objectives. Well-defined objectives should have three features according to Mager (1975). First, they should be relatively unambiguous, which is accomplished by choosing verbs which refer to readily observable behaviours such as write, list, mark or select from a list; rather than verbs describing mental states such as know, understand or appreciate. Second, 'the conditions of performance' should be known so that, for example, if the objective was that the student should be able to solve a mathematical problem it should be stipulated what aids he should be allowed to use. Similarly, if the objective was comprehension of written English, should dictionaries be allowed, should written or oral responses be required? Third, there should be clear guidelines as to the standard of performance, e.g., the percentage of correct responses, etc.

Ainscow and Tweddle recognize that this format is not appropriate for all curriculum material. They argue that it is most suitable for basic skill areas (number, reading, handwriting and language) for young children with learning difficulties. They are aware of some of the difficulties involved in writing behavioural objectives. Acceptable criteria levels are difficult to state unambiguously (e.g., in the case of shape drawing, what is an acceptable circle, square etc?). The solution to this is to produce more detailed descriptions of specific conditions and criteria, but this runs into the problem of how to operationalize unwieldy and unmanageable lists of objectives. Ainscow and Tweddle considered that a compromise could be found in most instances and that fairly specific but abbreviated lists of objectives were possible. The essential point to remember was that 'if specificity was to be sacrificed for the sake of brevity, the component which deals with the child's observable behaviour must be preserved. This is the essence of a behavioural objective' (p. 30). Another important point was that teachers who were to use the objectives should be brought into the discussions about conditions and criteria levels.

Once a carefully-graded sequence of behavioural objectives has been formulated, assessment can then have prescriptive consequences, because, unlike the old diagnostic labels and IQ scores, they relate to skills and achievements which the teacher is in a position to do something about. The teaching method is not necessarily unduly restricted by this approach. Although the objectives are clarified, the means to achieve them depend on the teacher's responding imaginatively and creatively to the specific circumstances. There are other advantages. Advocates claim that it encourages the spread of meaningul discussion between teachers who, by being forced to provide empirical referents for various abstract notions, thereby reveal exactly what they have in mind in a particular content area. Because objectives are clearly stated there are no great problems of evaluation. They form a starting point for curriculum development even if they are modified later and they assist in individualizing teaching. In general they help to make explicit what was previously implicit and they are an essential component of a rationally planned curriculum.

The implications for the EP of this approach are that: (a) it involves a considerable reduction of contact with individual children and an increase of contact with teachers; (b) it increases the

EP's effectiveness in disseminating psychological knowledge; (c) the number of individual referrals are reduced, the questions asked of the EP are more specific and there is no assumption that the child will be tested; (d) the discussion between teacher and EP is immediately about manipulating classroom behaviour rather than looking for causes 'within' the child.

Behaviour modification

In dealing with 'problem' behaviour using behaviour modification techniques, teachers are encouraged to forget about their preconceived notions of the non-ideal pupil, as well as all explanations involving factors within the child or influences from ouside the school, and to concentrate instead on detailed observation of the child's behaviour in the classroom and their own responses to that behaviour. Once the child's behaviour and their role in maintaining it have been clarified, it makes sense to think in terms of desired goals and the means of achieving them. The initial assessment stage is crucial because it represents the first attempts by the teacher to develop a different attitude. Leach and Raybould (1977) advise the teacher to observe behaviours 'objectively' in specific situations. Rather than use labels like 'withdrawn' or 'aggressive' to describe behaviours, teachers are advised that 'It is better to write "When observed by me on seven occasions I have never heard him speak to any other children" or "When observed by me I have seen him push one child in the back on four out of ten occasions" rather than "is withdrawn" or "is aggressive"' (p. 40). This will assist the teacher in viewing the problem 'objectively'.

Having clarified and defined the problem behaviour in this way, the next step is to establish what, if anything, should be done about it and this involves assessing the 'seriousness' of the problem. Again, rather than bringing in to play preconceived notions about 'seriousness', the teacher is asked to take a look at the behaviour 'objectively' which means that rather than evaluate it with reference to normative criteria he should, initially at any rate, provide a detailed description of the 'physical' parameters. For example, the teacher should note how long the behaviour lasts, how frequently it occurs and in how many situations it takes place. The next step is to plan the intervention. This involves rational planning in the form of a behavioural objectives approach:

(a) objectives are defined prior to teaching;

(b) objectives are identified in behavioural terms so that they can be readily observed and quantified;
(c) a carefully structured approach is then adopted with plenty of reinforcement; and
(d) the intervention is evaluated, a task which is made easier because base line behaviour and objectives have been clearly and precisely defined.

The basic principles of the behavioural approach here are essentially Skinnerian with the emphasis on reinforcement rather than punishment. A typical set of guidelines for teachers is provided by Becker *et al* (1967, p. 207):

1. Make explicit rules as to what is expected of children for each period.
2. Ignore (do not attend) behaviours which interfere with learning or teaching, unless a child is being hurt by another.
3. Give praise and attention to behaviours which facilitate learning. Tell the child what he is being praised for. Try to reinforce behaviours incompatible with those he wishes to decrease.

The only form of punishment suggested is the withdrawal of positive reinforcement.

THE APPEAL OF BEHAVIOURAL PSYCHOLOGY

What is it about the behavioural approach that leads psychologists who have some claim to be radically oriented to give it a measure of support? Dessent (1976), whose sympathies do not lie with the traditional paradigm, notes that the behaviour modification movement demands of EPs that they focus on the problem of the individual in the interactional setting where it is actually being experienced rather than from a distance in the isolation of a clinic or centre. Psychologists are thus compelled to work with teachers and parents and 'in so doing ... have been able to shed some of the trappings of the "visiting expert" role and the mystification element that was apparent in the traditional model with its implicit assumption that the psychologist had developed professional tools that he alone could understand and use' (p. 11).

There is even some support for behaviour modification from Hargreaves (1978). In his contribution to *Reconstructing Educational Psychology* (1978) he remarks that a behavioural psychologist 'has come some way from a medical model' and this has led him to an implicit critique of teachers, which for Hargreaves comes close to a 'more radical view that the "problem" could be located in the teacher rather than in the pupil' (p. 72). He also considers that 'educational psychologists have an impressive history of applying theory in ways that can be directly useful to teachers — one thinks of behaviour modification and microteaching . . . ' (p. 81).

Tizard (1976), another critic of the traditional paradigm, considers that behaviour modification techinques play an important part in giving a central role to the clarification of objectives and the evaluation of treatment programmes, a move which he clearly considers to be in a positive direction. They are also more desirable than 'dynamic models' because they are more effective in practice — even if they do only remove symptoms (Tizard, 1973).

Roe (1978) another contributor to the allegedly radically oriented *Reconstructing Educational Psychology* and whose general position, like that of Hargreaves, is not behaviourist, considers behaviour modification, like behaviour therapy, to have important advantages over the 'medical model'. He contrasts the behavioural model with the Freudian view — for the latter 'called dreams the royal road to the unconscious', whereas for the former and for those who disentangle themselves from the medical model 'Behaviour was the royal road to the child's world', and clearly a more relevant road for the EP. Behaviourism also helps practitioners to reject such vague terms as 'aggressive', 'withdrawn', 'school phobia', 'dyslexic', 'elective mute' and forces him to find out exactly what the child can or cannot do, on what occasions and under what circumstances.

All these authors are closely related to the practice of educational psychology — Roe and Dessent are practitioners, Hargreaves has addressed gatherings of EPs on numerous occasions and Tizard has frequently commented on psychological practice both in education and in the health service. All have some claim to be 'radical', even though their psychological and philosophical orientations differ.

A more consistent advocate of the behaviourist approach has been J. Presland. He is a practising Principal Educational Psychologist, who has made several contributions to the AEP *Journal* on the subject of behaviour modification both in relation to 'inappropriate' as well as 'academic' behaviour. In his 1972 article he contrasts the behavioural model with the medical model which he describes as 'traditional'. According to Presland, the medical model is one which views the problem behaviour as an 'illness' which can be 'cured' through 'therapy' — a model which underpins the notion of 'maladjustment' both in education and health settings. The medical model takes responsibility for his own cure away from the client or patient. In this respect, it is similar to what in previous chapters we have described as the 'traditional practitioner paradigm'. However, it is important to remember that although the traditional paradigm is frequently interpreted in a way which has consequences for practice which are similar to the medical model, it is not equivalent to the medical model in all its aspects. As we have seen, the discipline and profession of educational psychology developed a separate identity largely on the basis of the educationist's rejection of the medical model.

In general, the claim of the behavioural approach to be radical rests on three interrelated assumptions.

(a) It encourages the EP to investigate the problem in the interactional setting where it is situated, e.g., in the classroom.
(b) It is an approach which allows for more autonomy on the part of both teacher and pupil, and encourages them to take more responsibility for solving their own problems.
(c) It is an approach which avoids negative 'labelling' by a medical-type expert.

THE BEHAVIOURAL APPROACH IN ACTION

Behavioural Objectives

Although Ainscow and Tweddle stress that objectives must evolve from discussions with teachers if conditions and criteria for achievement are to be unambiguously formulated, it is doubtful if the problems of ambiguity can be completely overcome. According to Mager (1975) ambiguity can be reduced by the type of language used to describe objectives. Thus, verbs of action are preferred to verbs of state. This distinction is not in fact as clear cut as it may first appear. Clearly, 'covering with a card' is the former and 'to think critically' the latter, but what about 'to locate' or 'to connect' or even 'to select' or 'to choose'? It is often very difficult to decide whether a verb describes an observable behaviour or not. Attempts to reduce ambiguity may have a deleterious effect on the teaching/learning process by exaggerating the importance of the observable and thus, often, the more trivial aspects of the curriculum.

In discussions with educators, therefore, not all options are open as far as the behaviourally-oriented EP is concerned. Constraints are placed on 'free negotiations' by the latter's insistence on reducing ambiguity by specifying observables. Ainscow and Tweddle establish by fiat that this approach is applicable to basic skill areas, but educators may wish to argue the point.

Let us take the case of reading. From the behavioural viewpoint this is analysed in terms of behavioural skills. However it might, with some justification, be argued that highlighting observable skills, e.g., word recognition, results in a tendency to undervalue the linguistic and thinking powers that the child brings to the learning situation. Of course, the more difficult and complex aspects are not totally ignored in the behavioural approach. There is plenty of discussion of comprehensive and inferential 'skills' and language 'skills' are clearly considered important. But the stress on readily measurable and observable forms of these complex processes results in an emphasis on samples of behaviour which are inevitably oversimplified and narrow in terms of their intention to be representative of such processes.

Many progressive English teachers consider this to be a typical feature of the psychologist's approach. In their eyes psychologists seem to have become totally identified with the behavioural approach. McKenzie in Rosen (1975) remarks that '... the notion that reading is an extension of language, that the child is a constructive, powerful learner seems to be abandoned and the psychologists take over with their theory that learning to read is a logical, sequential process' p. 21. Not all behaviouralists, in fact, make this claim, but many do.

In short, the behavioural approach is not based on a view of learning which is informed by the principle that reading is a 'thinking process' (see Morris, 1963) and therefore should be taught right from the start as a positive aid to reflection on experience. Many behavioural intervention strategies in reading are based on a Skinnerian approach, which increases the likelihood of fragmetation still further by demanding that every small step be reinforced. Psychologists adopting this approach often completely lose sight of what is and what is not important in learning to read. To give an American example: in a study by Staats and Butterfield (1965) a boy is consistently reinforced for 'maintenance of attention towards the printed word'. It could be argued, however, that if a child is reading and thinking, a shift of attention at regular intervals might represent a temporary but necessary withdrawal in order to reflect on what has been read.

Another aspect of negotiations with teachers in which the behaviourally-oriented EP shows distinct limitations is in relation to the question of curriculum content. The behavioural approach does not tackle the problem of the origins of objectives — why is that particular area of knowledge from which objectives are to be derived important to teach; what assumptions are made about the nature of education and the learning process; who decides what is to be taught? MacDonald Ross (1973) says: 'This evasion amounts to a truncation of the process of planning — chopping off the normative and strategic levels and concentrating on operational issues' (p. 20).

Of course, it is possible for EPs to stipulate the curriculum content that they consider to be important, e.g., reading, before tackling the task of producing teachable objectives. However, it is more likely that the EP's influence on content will be a result of 'backwash' from his efforts to operationalize objectives. In either case the methodology does not encourage him to spend much time discussing many of those curriculum issues which teachers consider to be important. Many teachers like to state objectives in terms of constructs (e.g., self-confidence), regarding observables as indicators from which the presence of characteristics described by the construct can be inferred. Cronbach (1971) acknowledges the anticipatory nature of constructs which preclude their being totally specifiable in the here and now: '... no list of specific responses-to-situations, however lengthy can define the construct, since the construct is intended to apply to situations that will arise in the future but cannot be specified now.'

As MacDonald Ross points out the guiding procedural philosophy involved here is 'operationalism'. He quotes Bridgeman (1927): 'The concept of length involves as much as and nothing more than the set of operations by which length is determined.' One is instantly reminded of intelligence testing — 'intelligence is what intelligence tests measure' and the positivist view of science.

Assessment based on a behavioural objectives model, therefore, has a tendency to narrow the focus of the educator too quickly on too simplistically conceived operational issues. Although discussions and negotiations with teachers are considered a necessary part of the procedure, a typical description of the approach in action usually underplays the more complex aspects of the school and classroom 'milieu' (see Hamilton, 1976) in which the formal curricular activities are located. The importance of this lies in the fact that, despite the great efforts to be precise in defining objectives, the overall impact on remediation processes is rather 'hit and miss'. Failure to take into account crucial aspects of the milieu results in various outcomes which in many cases could have been anticipated by a more 'exploratory' approach to appraisal and evaluation. An important feature of the milieu which is often neglected by the ardent behaviouralist is the interaction effect between pupils and teachers which results in objectives being reinterpreted and altered in midstream. Of course, behaviouralists are usually aware that this might happen, but insist that it does nothing to detract from the desirability of at least starting off with a list of pre-specified objectives. But why devote so much energy to this, inevitably, extremely arduous and time-consuming exercise when objectives are usually going to be altered, either in minor or major ways? The main thrust of the behavioural objectives model seems to involve just as much emphasis on spurious attempts at precision as the psychometric approach.

Behaviour modification

The point of intervention

Just as the behavioural objectives approach does not tackle the question of the origins of objectives, so behaviour modification techniques provide few guidelines as to exactly where the EP's intervention should be. Because their main concern is the techniques of behavioural observation and the creation and evaluation of programmes, behaviouralists do not attempt a serious analysis of why some children and not others are selected for observation in the first place. As noted earlier, one strategy used by behaviouralists is to obtain a rating of the 'seriousness' of the problem by asking teachers to rate in an 'objective' fashion the physical, temporal and spatial aspects of the behaviour concerned. Values are clearly involved in the assumption that these features are important. Even so the word 'objective' does seem partly justified since such behaviours can be reliably observed. However, these dimensions of behaviours are rarely sufficient by themselves to indicate 'seriousness' and they usually have to be supplemented by other measures, the 'objectivity' of which is less easily justified. Usually, teachers are asked whether they consider the behaviour to be 'normal' for a child of that age or whether they feel the behaviour is 'reasonable'.

Of course, what is 'normal' or 'reasonable' behaviour is problematic and this point is usually recognized by psychologists. Many would agree with Chazan *et al* (1974) '... success and failure in learning are relative concepts and terms such as "dull", "backward", "subnormal" or "retarded" do not have precise scientific meaning; their connotations are affected by such factors as the population being studied and the skills under consideration.' For Leach and Raybould behavioural deviance is a relative concept: 'It depends both on the nature of the child's situation and on the 'coping' levels of the adults who have to deal with him' (op. cit. p. 145). The idea of relativity leads to an emphasis on the importance of the teacher's definition of the problem because in a sense there is a problem if the teacher thinks there is one. However, since the problem can also be a function of the 'nature of the child's situation', which the teacher does not always appreciate, i.e., does not regard as constituting a problem, the behavioural psychologist usually has to introduce a behavioural 'yardstick' derived from normative criteria against which the child's behaviour can be evaluated. This can take the form of a diagnosis using norm-referenced tests administered by an EP, but more typically, in keeping with the perspective of giving teachers more responsibility, it takes the form of a behavioural check-list provided by the EP but completed by the teacher. Rather than being imposed on the teacher, the check-list serves as a 'negotiating instrument' which enables the EP and the teacher to arrive at some form of agreement as to the definition of the situation, e.g., whether a particular behaviour is 'serious' enough to warrant intervention by the EP. In this way the EP may hope to 'sensitize' the teacher to certain problems which she may otherwise ignore.

The question, then, is where do the items of the check-list come from? The EP, because he appreciates the nature of the 'field' in which his check-list will be used, will take into account the need to include items which relate to an educational context. He may even include items suggested by teachers. He will also select items which are likely to be reliable, such as observable behaviours. But in practice also he will draw on his esoteric knowledge — his knowledge of psychological theory and research and particularly of child development studies.

An example of a check-list currently employed by psychologists in several LEAs is the Croydon Check List, which was noted by Bullock as a useful method of screening and identifying learning problems early. It contains items relating to:

1. speech-communication, e.g., retains and transmits simple messages;
2. perceptual-motor, e.g., can reproduce shapes;
3. emotional/social, e.g., integration with peers in learning situations and appropriate relationships with peers. and
4. response to learning-situation, e.g., eager to learn.

This check-list is quoted with approval by Raybould and Leach.

The link between the check-list and behavioural strategies of intervention is made quite clear by the author (Wolfendale, 1976, p. 111). Structured intervention would ensue, e.g., 'exercises and activities covering the development of listening skills, use and understanding of words and concepts, flexibility of thought, and expressive skills' and behaviour modification principles would be used for helping 'children manifesting behavioural and emotional difficulties which may interfere with learning' (p. 112).

The Croydon items contain some which are school specific, but most items are fairly familiar to psychologists and recognizable as the kinds of behaviours usually contained in intelligence tests and developmental measures. Many of the items, such as 'retains and transmits simple messages', are similar to intelligence test items, and the division of the 'whole' child into sets of language, motor and social-emotional skills is typical of positivist developmental psychology. An EP using this check-list as a means of deciding upon his point of intervention is therefore using criteria from psychometric tests and developmental psychology. Thus, although he claims not to be interested in a psychology concerned with 'within child' factors, he cannot seem to avoid some reference to the norms derived from this psychology as an essential prerequisite of his rationally-planned behavioural strategy.

A close look at most applications of behavioural techinques usually reveals that a number of assumptions derived from psychometrics and developmental psychology, either implicitly or explicitly, are acting as a framework for practice by providing criteria for the selection of 'cases' as well as providing the performance goals which the programme is designed to achieve. Leach and Raybould, for example, refer to 'maladaptive' behaviours as if this were unproblematic. It is clearly not self-evident as to what constitutes 'maladaptive' or 'adaptive' behaviour unless one accepts that this has already been established by research in child development. This research typically acts as an important background reference point for behaviouralists. Thus, though Skinner (1974) considered that the source of differences between students was not important, he referred to the fact that 'difference in the rate at which students work may be genetic or environmental and probably both' (p. 200)!

Pupil and teacher autonomy

On the face of it behaviour modification does not seem a technique conducive to the furtherance of 'freedom' in teacher–pupil relationships and of the individual responsibility that goes with it. It is hard to imagine a more 'oppressive' relationship than one where a teacher attempts to control a pupil's behaviour by assuming that the pupil's conciousness is not important and provides rewards or punishment in the same way as he might do when training a dog. Not only is the child 'depersonalized' in this situation and treated as a 'dependent variable', but the teacher is also restricted in his responses and has to confine his contact with the child to a basic 'carrot and stick' level. The degrees of freedom are thus limited for both parties and it is as depersonalizing for the teacher as it is for the child.

Two examples will suffice to demonstrate the point. Blackham and Silberman (1971) refer to Burns (1970) who 'attempted to change the behaviour of an effeminate third grade boy. The teacher was encouraged to smile and verbally reinforce the child when he played with male peers and to ignore him when he played with girls . . . When the child talked about masculine activities, the counsellor would display interest, but he would ignore the boy when he expressed feminine interests' (p. 63).

Woody (1968) describes the behavioural approach to counselling as action oriented (as opposed to insight oriented) and based on the principles of learning theory. He gives a fictitious example of a boy coming to the counsellor because he wants to talk about getting a job on leaving school. The counsellor takes this at face value and immediately sets up the behavioural goal as 'making a vocational choice' any moves towards which are reinforced. If the boy seems to stray from the point, no reinforcement is given, i.e., the counsellor remains silent. And so when the boy says 'I started to ask my mum what she thought, but she had to go off to the hospital for a check-up. She's been sick you know', the counsellor remains silent in order not to 'reinforce responses unrelated to the matter of vocational choice'. The fact that the boy might have been extremely worried about his mother's health is not acknowledged by the counsellor because superficially it appears to have no relevance to the matter in hand.

In neither of these examples does the counsellor demonstrate that he has even attempted to get to grips with the difficult task of arriving at some understanding of the pupil's own conception of his problems and aspirations.

However, it is fair to say that proponents of behaviour modification techniques have shown themselves to be aware of the need to avoid applying them indiscriminately and insensitively. Like many others, Meacham and Wiesen (1969) regard these techniques as compatible with a humanistic position. They deny that their approach is too cold and does not allow 'for the emotional growth of the individual student' because their ideas are derived from a philosophy called 'humanistic behaviourism which offers the greatest promise for the education of students who will have to run a complex technological society but who must understand that basic human needs should dictate the course of technological development'.

In many behaviour modification programmes the only form of punishment suggested is the withdrawal of positive reinforcement. This, according to behavioural psychologists, meets the first humanist objection that behaviour modification tends to emphasize punishment and overtly coercive measures rather than reward. The second objection often voiced by humanist critics is that these techniques are too manipulative. They tend to be imposed on the child without his knowledge and are carried out irrespective of his wishes. Many behaviour modification techniques, however, involve a contract between teacher and child which implies that: (a) the child's consent is obtained; and (b) the child knows what is taking place. In fact, as Leach and Raybould (1977) point out, the ultimate aim of behavioural modification is not external behavioural control but self-management, self-direction and self-regulation. Some behavioural modification programmes are directed by the child himself — he records his behaviour and rewards himself.

Nevertheless, the behavioural approach to 'deviant' behaviour, as with the teaching of reading, is in the final analysis diametrically opposed to many humanistic principles. Behaviour modification is based on a completely different model of the child, the teacher and their interaction. Although the child's perspective may be taken into account initially, most programmes in their implementation are teacher controlled and do not involve open, dialectical teacher–pupil relationships. Even when attempts are made to allow the child to direct his own programme, the model of the school context employed is usually over-simplified, too superficial and takes too much for granted. For example, there is very little concern for some of the more subtle features of socio-educational processes, e.g., the 'hidden curriculum' which might enable the teacher to retain a manipulatory role even when the programme is supposedly self-regulated by the pupil. The fact that self-regulation 'skills' have to be specially taught (see Leach and Raybould, 1977) attests to the fact that they are not intrinsic to such programmes, as they would be to a humanistic approach.

A third humanist objection to behaviour modification is that the teacher is also 'depersonalized' in the process. This is countered by pointing out that teachers are brought into the discussions on strategies at every stage of their formulation. Indeed, it would be regarded as a waste of time not to include them, because it is they who would be implementing the programmes. The fact that strategies and programmes are negotiated between teachers and

EPs attests to the fact that both these practitioners are viewed as relatively autonomous agents with responsibilities rather than as determined and depersonalized objects.

And yet a careful examination of some of the more popular descriptions of behaviour modification techniques applied to education suggests that behaviourally-oriented EPs often base their intervention strategy on an invalidation of the teacher view. Leach and Raybould (1977), for example, insist that it is important for teachers to make sure their judgements are 'realistic' by which they mean based on behavioural data. If they do this, they have a chance of reducing 'the attitudinal and affective sets . . . which can bias perception' (p. 40). In this instance teacher perceptions of children are not being regarded as a 'normal' function of social and psychological circumstances but as 'distorted' in the same way that a psychologist would regard certain views held by his patients or clients as not in tune with the reality principle. Basically, teachers' perceptions of problems are seen as mistaken or derived from a biased view of what is 'really' the case.

CONCLUSION — THE RADICAL CLAIMS OF THE BEHAVIOURAL APPROACH

We are now in a position to assess to what extent the behavioural approach represents a radical break with tradition. First, does it encourage the EP to investigate the problem in the interactional setting? Yes, but it is a limited model for this purpose. If it leads to curriculum-based assessment, it also results in an emphasis on behavioural objectives. The latter seems almost as restrictive as the traditional psychometric approach. It does not really enable the EP to get to grips with the complexities of the classroom, or base his procedures on a model of learning which takes into account socially generated meanings.

Second, does the approach encourage teachers and pupils to take more responsibility for their own problems? Although given a humanistic gloss, behavioural approaches do not seem to be based on principles which inherently involve self-regulation by pupils or teacher–pupil relationships characterized by mutual respect for individual freedom and the maximization of autonomy.

Third, is deviant labelling avoided and is the EP less of a visiting expert? It is unlikely that it is any different from the traditional paradigm in this respect because:
(a) A child can be 'negatively' labelled in behavioural terms, e.g., a child who refused to co-operate in a behaviour modification

programme might be described as 'lacking social skills'. Of course, it can be argued, in a rather naive fashion, that the behavioural approach encourages description of the behaviour rather than labelling of the person. But if generalizations about persons who repeatedly behave in certain ways can be avoided, then this is surely possible to do within frameworks provided by other psychological models and is not peculiar to the behavioural approach. We can refer to 'defence mechanisms', for example, and at the same time be wary about making unwarranted generalizations about the person.

(b) The fact that a child is selected in the first place for a behavioural programme means that he is possibly already 'negatively' labelled.

(c) In so far as the point of intervention is decided upon by a score on a check-list the labels are likely to be reinforced by traditional esoteric knowledge. The EP introduces knowledge from psychometrics and developmental studies as well as behaviourist learning theories, and therefore knowledge which is to some extent his speciality thus his expertise. The fact that the behavioural approach involves more interaction with teachers does nothing to detract from this. Psychotherapists work closely with clients but this does not mean they relinquish the image of a professional with special knowledge. It is true that the behavioural approach is likely to make him more visible, more accessible, more flexible, more open to feedback and therefore probably more accountable and open to criticism. He may even construe his role as one where his relationships with teachers and indeed parents are on an equal and democratic basis. But all this is unlikely to be radically different from the low profile expertism of the traditional paradigm.

CHAPTER 7

Sociological and radical alternatives

The non-directive style and the behavioural approach were the responses of some EPs to changing circumstances. Although the 'broad concept of special education' had always guided developments in Britain, it was not until the mid 1960s that the idea was implemented on anything like the scale that was required (but see Booth, 1981). EPs had always carried out advisory work in ordinary schools with children in the 'normal' and 'special' ranges, but the 'broad concept of special education' employed by Warnock required that more emphasis should be given to understanding the school context. EPs wanted to know the details of what was actually taking place in classrooms in relation to individual children 'at risk', and teachers, if they were to retain 'special' children in the ordinary classroom, required more advice, support and practical suggestions.

As we have seen, non-directiveness and behaviouralism were steps in the right direction. They involved giving more responsibility to the teacher and the school, and put the emphasis on school factors rather than 'within child' explanations. However, they were strategies which helped the EP to adapt to changing circumstances in a way that enabled him to retain his identity under the umbrella of the traditional practitioner paradigm, broadly defined; that is, without having to surrender his professional image of 'scientist' which was important for his credibility in relation to other professionals. Thus, the behavioural approach was presented as applied psychological science. It was, like the non-directive style, based on an intra-paradigmic shift rather than a complete change of paradigm.

These adaptations within the existing paradigm were not, however, the only options available and towards the end of the 'seventies attempts were made to create a genuine alternative by 'reconstructing' educational psychology towards a more sociologically-oriented view of theory and practice.

THE SOCIOLOGICAL ORIENTATION

Since one of the hallmarks of traditional practice had been its tendency to favour psycho-biological explanations, an alternative practice would seem to be one that was derived from a knowledge base that was 'fully social'. In the second half of the 'seventies two approaches emerged which were potentially appropriate in this respect. One was derived from a 'systems', the other from an 'interactionist' perspective.

The 'systems' approach

In his overview of 'systems theory' Burden (1981) considers that the 'sociological perspective' helps us to look at school processes in a way that produces information that might well be overlooked by psychologists. After briefly reviewing a number of theories of organization he lists three implications for practice carried out by a 'systems engineer' EP. First, we start at the insitutional rather than individual level and work from the assumption that 'many examples of behaviour described as disruptive or problematical by those working within a position of authority in schools can be viewed as problems of the schools themselves rather than of individuals or "society" ' (page 35). Second, we need to understand how the explicit and implicit organizational structure of a school influences pupils' perception and behaviour in a way that teachers regard the pupils as problems: i.e., we need to understand *processes*. Third, and crucially,

> The school needs to be seen as an open system in constant dynamic interaction with the environment that it serves ... Its success will be viewed according to how well it maintains an internal state of equilibrium whilst adapting to the ever-changing needs of society and therefore of its [the school's] products ... Systems theory argues that dynamic tension is a potentially positive rather than negative sign, providing that the necessary feedback mechanisms are operating effectively within the system in order to implement a required balancing-out effect. (page 36)

This approach certainly encourages the EP to take a much broader view. For example, rather than spending his time interviewing individual children with remedial problems, he is likely to become more involved in exercises which attempt to evaluate the whole of the remedial provision in the school. He will perhaps attempt to help the teachers to clarify the aims and objectives of this provision, and to assess how the remedial 'system' articulates with other 'systems' in the school, e.g., pastoral care and subject deparments. As a result he might express concern about the lack of common aims and poor communication between departments which makes for inefficiency and wasteful expenditure of energy. His recommendations might include innovations in the curricular activities of various departments, suggestions as to ways of making and maintaining links between departments and advice about monitoring and evaluating the changes. In the process of assisting the school in this way his special input might have included his expertise in assessment and his understanding of remedial techniques, but his overriding concern will have been to apply his knowledge of systems theory and to stress the need to perceive the school as an organic whole composed of sub-systems in need of rationalization and integration. He will most probably, of course, not have been working alone, but as a member of a systems team. At some point, he might, for one reason or another, talk to staff about or even interview one or two individual children, but, as Burden recommends, he will have started at the institutional level.

The second strength of this approach is that it stresses the notion that schools are open systems, i.e., organizations which cannot be viewed in isolation from the 'environment' in which they are located. This means that the relationships of the school to the wider society must be considered, e.g., the family, the community, political and cultural institutions, industry etc., and that this be viewed as a 'dynamic interaction'. Such a model opens the way for some interesting analyses of the relationship between, say, changes in schools and changes in the political and economic structures. One might find, for example, that there had been a certain amount of 'system drift' in schools as a result of subsystems adapting to changing economic circumstances outside schools. Thus, in a situation of high youth unemployment, a course on social studies becomes a course on 'life and communication' skills relating specifically to employability and the original aims and objectives of the course are subtly altered. This is a use of systems theory in what Perrow (1979) describes as the exposé tradition. The explanation of 'system drift' is in terms of systems making efforts to ensure their own survival in a changing environment.

It is in this last sentence that we can see some of the possible weaknesses of systems theory as far as the change-oriented EP is concerned. Having broken with the biologism of a positivist and individualist knowledge base, he is in danger of adopting a social perspective which is founded on a view of the social system as a biological organism! The school is conceived as a system with survival needs of its own. What individual and psychological entities are doing is much the same as what social systems are doing. Feedback mechanisms are operating in each case to achieve balancing out effects bringing the individual or social organism back to a state of equilibrium and thus helping it to survive.

Moreover, although the change-oriented EP probably wishes to start at the institutional level, this does not mean that he is not interested in the individual consciousness of teachers and pupils in schools. As Burden indicates one is interested in the way social structures influence people's perceptions. But what does systems theory offer as a model of the person? In general, it conceives of the person either as a blank sheet to be 'filled' in the way the system requires, i.e., a programmed role player, or as a 'personality' imported into the system. Individuals enter the system not with identities that have been socially constructed but as psychobiological entities who differ individually very much in the manner that positivist psychology would predict. This version of the open systems approach is typical of EPs who attempt to work in alternative ways but still wish to cling to the old paradigm. It is expressed in the form of an attempted synthesis of the systems approach with the traditional knowledge base. Thus Galloway (1981), at the end of a chapter entitled 'Institutional Change or Individual Change? An Overview', concludes that: 'This chapter is an attempt to synthesize the most useful aspects of a systems approach with those of a child centred approach *focusing on individual differences*' (p. 168).

Another problem with the open systems approach is that, particularly in the hands of practitioners who have traditionally been concerned with the individual or 'micro' social level, there is a tendency for the links between the system in focus, i.e., the school, and the wider system to be underinvestigated. Thus, as Dale (1972) points out, even those who advocate an open system approach often do not adhere to it. People have identities outside organizations which influence the way they perform their roles within organizations. These identities relate to other systems, which cannot therefore easily be ignored in a systems analysis. External systems (e.g. class, religious, political) influence social relations in schools at every level from pupil motivation and staff ideologies to the content of the curriculum and the 'ecology' of the school. This is what is meant by dynamic interaction and it raises questions as to whether the school can be viewed as a socioloigically separate unit under any circumstances and, if it can, whether the tightness and integration conjured up by the notion of organism is appropriate.

Of course, advocates of the systems approach would probably deny that the idea of a school as an organism was anything other than an interesting analogy providing a readily understood, shorthand description of a certain type of structure. A sympathetic view of the EP as systems engineer would see him as merely utilizing the rhetoric of systems theory as a way of justifying his involvement with schools at the institutional level. As far as the practitioner is concerned, therefore, the important question is whether or not the systems model helps him to come to grips with the problems that arise when he attempts to work in alternative ways. Does it help to illuminate how the schools which he serves operate? Are the areas which it encourages him to focus on relevant? It seems to me that there are tendencies inherent in this approach which lead to the underemphasis of aspects of social life in schools which the change-oriented EP would consider to be crucial.

One example of this is the tendency to play down the role of conflicting perspectives within the organization. The 'neutral' state of affairs for the systems analyst is for there to be a consensus over goals and values. When this consensus is threatened by conflict, then he would stress the desirability and necessity of a speedy resolution of conflict and re-establishment of the consensus.

But, as every practising EP knows, many conflicts in school are not so easily and quickly resolved. Undue haste to re-establish a consensus (assuming that one existed in the first place) can result in action based on a superficial and 'phoney' agreement on educational objectives. Examples of this are often to be found in rationalization programmes based on network analyses of explicit and formal rather than implicit and informal role functions (see for example Richardson, 1973).

Another tendency of the systems approach is to focus on official rather than unofficial systems. Thus while there is plenty of discussion and analysis of the relationships between the various subject and other departments, there is less interest shown in examining the 'hidden curriculum' or the pupil culture. This basically derives from a failure to appreciate the importance of understanding the group perspectives of all the participants. Schools are looked at essentially from a managerial viewpoint, but although this is an interesting and significant perspective it is clearly not the only one which the EP needs to take into account. He is not just concerned with the efficiency of the system 'as she is spoke', but with prior questions such as how one defines efficiency, and efficient for whom?

These tendencies, plus the one referred to earlier concerning the lack of analysis of the interaction between school and the wider society, can be seen at work in Burden's (1978) description of a project-centred approach based on a systems analysis. Up to a point this is a laudable attempt to develop an alternative practice. There is not sufficient space for a detailed analysis, but a few quotations will suffice to demonstrate the main thrust of the approach. Burden admits that there may be some difficulty in obtaining a consensus on objectives. Rather than exploring the causes of this, he views the situation as one which the systems engineer should clearly not tolerate for long: 'However great the resistance to the formulation of objectives and the establishment of quantifiable critera, this stage is essential in order to monitor efficiency' (p. 121). He quotes Jenkins with approval: ... 'The systems approach to problems is a way of replacing a piecemeal approach by one that attempts to look at problems in their overall context' (p. 118). However, his project-centred approach does not in fact involve an analysis of the 'overall context'. There is at one point in his description of the CIPP (Context, Input, Process and Product) analysis a recommendation that we start by defining the context — 'the environment where change is to occur' — and we are exhorted to take into account the 'environment's unmet needs', but these needs are not seriously discussed anywhere. There is also a passing reference to the 'wider consideration of the issue of compulsory comprehensive education and its effect on the attitude of the school staff and the local population' (p. 121). Again, one searches in vain for an analysis of these attitudes and the group perspectives in which they are rooted.

The interactionist perspective

The second main sociologically-oriented alternative to the traditional paradigm is the interactionist perspective. According to Blumer (1969) 'symbolic interactionism' is based on three simple premises: (a) 'that human beings act towards things on the basis of the meaning the things have for them'; (b) that the meanings originate in social interaction and (c) meanings can be altered by interpretative processes as social action proceeds. A thing or an object is anything that can be indicated, i.e., pointed to or referred to, such as physical objects, abstract objects (e.g., moral principles) or social objects, usually people.

A central construct of symbolic interactionism is the self. The self is a social object and a person can make indications to his own self. He can refer to himself and can act on the basis of how he perceives himself, that is on the basis of the meaning of the self. As with other objects, the meaning of the self emerges in the process of social interaction. The person can take on the role of the 'other' and look at himself from another's point of view. The expectations of others thus play an important part in constructing the identity of the person. But the person is not an automaton. Up to a point, he is free to choose which definition of the self he will accept. Socially generated meanings that groups of people share are called 'cultures'. A culture consists of ready-made interpretations embodied in linguistic and other symbols which are available to a person who shares these meanings. Many of these shared meanings influence the taken-for-granted rules which actors have constructed in order to resolve problems with which they are faced. Individuals are often unaware or only partially aware of these rules which structure everyday life (analogous to speaking language without being aware of the rules of grammar). In schools there are a large number of rules and routines which a newcomer has to learn, but which are taken for granted by participants. However, although life in schools as elsewhere is founded on rules, there are large areas of ambiguity, lack of clarity and lack of agreement about the nature of the rules and their appropriate application.

Social life is thus conceived as a web of negotiation with people interpreting and reinterpreting objects and events in accordance with their definitions of the situation, and perceived interests. Lines of action are drawn up which reflect these interpretations and create a patterning of interaction based on a negotiated order. Power is defined as the ability to impose your definition of the situation. If actors or participants are equally matched power-wise there is likely to be more negotiation than if power is distributed asymmetrically.

Deviance is action which breaks cultural rules, and which is interpreted by members as so doing. People who break rules regularly are at risk of becoming labelled as deviant and may as a result of this come to see themselves as deviant. A label is a construct or typification which is usually part of a system or scheme of constructs. Typifications, like rules, help to order and structure the social world in order to make it more predictable and orderly. For a typification to be of use in this way it must be relevant to the specific context of interaction as defined by the actors.

Once a person has been labelled certain consequences follow from this. Not all labelling has negative consequences. The problem with deviant labelling is that it is stigmatizing and thus creates problems for the person labelled. It can lead to a person labelling himself as a deviant on a permanent basis and following a deviant career path with little hope of his identity being reinterpreted either by himself or by others.

This brief sketch of the vocabulary of interactionism is sufficient to indicate the richness of this perspective as a resource for an alternative psychological practice. Unlike the systems approach it provides a useful framework for understanding the different views and perceptions of school among pupils and teachers, and how these effect ongoing social life in schools. It also provides conceptual tools for analysing the rationale and consequences of the EP's involvement with individual 'problem' children. In general, the approach seems to represent a way of genuinely synthesizing work at the institutional and individual level. The individual's needs are seen as socially constructed and the institution is not perceived as an impersonal monolithic structure but a series of relatively permanent social arrangements continually being subjected to negotiation and interpretation by participants. Concepts like self, identity, labelling, culture, rules, typifications, stigma, negotiation and power all necessitate an approach to practice which must be based on an analysis of the 'fine grain' of social processes, thus continually pushing the EP in the direction of 'where the action is'. He cannot ignore conflicts of perspective, the hidden curriculum, pupil culture or individual consciousness because these are at the very heart of an interactionist analysis. At the same time he can cope with consensus and order via terms like negotiation and power.

SOME IMPLICATIONS OF THE INTERACTIONIST PERSPECTIVE FOR PRACTICE

The interactionist perspective promotes a certain kind of sensitivity among EPs about the nature of labelling and its possible consequences. The solution is not to totally avoid labelling, because clearly labelling in its broadest sense (i.e., categorization) is a pervasive phenomenon of social life. But the EP should be concerned about the nature of the labels he is using and the possible consequences of applying them to children who are considered to present problems for the education system. Unless he is aware of these processes, he could be instrumental in applying labels which are stigmatizing and have negative consequences for the child. The difficulty is that for many EPs, particularly those still influenced by the traditional paradigm, the labels they use not only appear harmless but have actually often resulted in something positive being done for the child in terms of his future psychological and educational development. Thus intelligence testing, when it was introduced in the early part of the century, did much to prevent children with below average and average intelligence being placed in institutions outside the normal education system because of backwardness in basic attainments. In a sense, one label, like IQ, was used to prevent another label, like ineducable, being applied, and it is quite clear which of these would have been the more stigmatizing.

What the interactionist perspective does is to continually force the labelling issue on to the agenda. The question is not whether certain labels are inherently stigmatizing or 'negative' in their consequences, but rather what is the role of labels in the specific social and historical circumstances in which they are used. I have assumed in this book that there is enough evidence to show that the labels of the traditional paradigm in the recent past and in the current period do not, on the whole, result in positive educational consequences.

In the first place, traditional labelling has contributed to the formation of teacher expectations which have tended to underestimate the educational potential of many children. Second, it has provided a rationale for placing children in special environments in an historical period where there has been an increasing concern for 'normalization'. Third, because it has pretensions to being 'scientific' and 'neutral' not sufficient attention has been paid to how these labels articulate with cultural forms in the wider society. The dilemma for the EP, therefore, is that, when he accepts a referral, he does not know whether his involvement is contributing to the stabilization of a deviant identity or is the beginning of a de-labelling process. The mere fact of child X being referred to the EP may be sufficient to 'harden' the kind of identity which can only be counterproductive in the long term for both the child and society.

It is clearly imperative for the EP to have some understanding of the situation before he intervenes, that is even before he accepts a referral. He must have pre-referral discussions with teachers, attempt to assess the climate of opinion about the child and arrive at some understanding of the social and psychological factors which precipitated the referral. This, of course, can be exasperating for the teachers who requested the referral. They may have persevered with the problem doggedly until the point was reached where they felt that outside help was needed, only to be told that the situation had to be fully explored with the EP before a referral could even be accepted. Nevertheless, there is no alternative to this process if the possible dangers of labelling are to be taken seriously. In practice, many teachers are fully appreciative of the EP's dilemma here and it is possible for an EP to strike up a relationship with a school where referrals are 'negotiated'. Such negotiations will vary from school to school and from situation to situation. There may be some schools where the cultural climate and organization is such that nothing other than a traditional referral model can be negotiated. In such schools, it seems to me that there is a strong case for the EP not accepting any individual referrals at all, unless by doing so he can eventually change the basis of his involvement with the school.

However, although individual referrals are not completely ruled out in the event of the EP deciding to adopt an interactionist perspective, there is a case, even in schools where referrals are negotiated, for the creation of a non-referral model as the normal mode of interaction between school and EP. This model is referred to in a paper summarizing a discussion among psychologists of a paper written by David Hargreaves entitled 'The deviant pupil in the secondary school' (DECP, 1976).

> The thoroughgoing answer to the problems posed by participating in the referral system is simply not to — to base contact with a school and discussion of the educational and psychological possibilities and problems on a series of regular, possibly three-weekly visits and continue this whether a school refers any children or not. (p. 555)

This opens up the possibility of EPs expanding their role in the manner envisaged by some of the early pioneers of the school psychological service. Children could still be seen but on an informal basis either individually or in groups. What else might this broad conception of role involve? A whole range of activities are possible, many of which are already carried out by EPs in one form or another, but in the non-referral model they would become central and regular rather than marginal and intermittent. The EP could involve himself in curriculum innovation and evaluation, in developing pastoral care or remedial procedures, in school based in-service training, in home–school liaison, etc. The special contribution of the EP in these areas would, of course, involve 'knowledge' from the interactionist perspective. The two examples which follow will suffice.

In-service training

Teachers sensitized to labelling processes might wish to know what, if anything, can be done to avoid deviant labelling and its negative consequences. An introduction to and critical appreciation of Hargreaves' (1978) prescriptions might provide a useful starting point. This author suggests that since deviance is rule breaking, if schools reduce the number of rules then they would automatically reduce the amount of rule breaking. He gives the example of rules about long hair for boys. Nowadays, in many schools there are no rules about this and therefore to have long hair is not to break a rule and therefore not to commit a deviant act. Of course, since schools are rule-bound institutions there must be some rules and therefore inevitably some deviance, but rules can be kept down to a minimum and the irrelevant and unnecessary ones cut out.

Teachers might well react by criticizing this prescription. Even if unnecessary rules were abolished no doubt pupils bent on deviance would find some rules to break, and in any case rules which could be abolished are few and marginal rather than central to the maintenance of order in the institution. However, the importance of the interactionist perspective here is not that it might help to reveal rules which could be abolished but that it encourages all concerned to examine what rules are actually operating in the school and this is a worthy exercise in itself. A discussion about rules is one of the most promising techniques for helping teachers to reflect on their roles and their ideas about teaching. It helps to expose many of the taken-for-granted aspects of school life. It also helps the EP to achieve an increased understanding of the 'hidden curriculum' of the school so that if he does have to see individual children on a referral or non-referral basis his assessments and recommendations can be made relevant to the specific situation.

The scrutiny of rules in school is not a superficial exercise. It might be so if carried out under the auspices of the traditional paradigm or from the management viewpoint of the systems approach, but from the interactionist perspective it involves taking a very long hard look at some of the more complex and ambiguous features of school life. The rules under examination involve more than just what are commonly known as school rules, such as no running in the corridor, no playing football near the school greenhouse. They also include the informal, situational, personal and often unarticulated rules which are peculiar to interaction in a particular classroom and may or may not be generalized beyond this arena. For example, as Hargreaves *et al* (1975) noted, there are scores of rules relating to the 'fine grain' of classroom interaction — rules about talk, movement, time, teacher–pupil and pupil–pupil relationships — of which teachers often are only half aware, but will acknowledge if their attention is drawn to them. Teachers vary in the number of rules they negotiate, the type of rules, the way they apply them and how often they apply them. Some teachers are more concerned than others about implementing rules based on moral principles, e.g., thou shalt not address the teacher in a certain manner because that is not a proper way for children to address adults. Others are more pragmatic in their approach and are more concerned that the lesson should flow and learning take place than that a moral point should be made. Pupils also take many rules for granted. Sometimes they are unclear as to whether or not a rule is in play or they are not sure if the teacher has noticed a case of rule breaking. The ebb and flow of activity and experience in the classroom has to be interpreted by both pupil and teacher. These processes have to be acknowledged and reflected upon if the persons involved are to achieve self-understanding and produce meaningful changes in practice.

Hargreaves' second recommendation is that teachers should attempt to label the act rather than the person.

> This separation of act from person is crucial, for only then can the labeller indicate to the offender that his acts are discrepant and incongruent with himself, and thus provide him with the social support that will encourage the offender to give up the acts as they are inconsistent with both his own self conception and the identity the labeller imputes to him. (p. 19)

Again teachers may find this an easy target for criticism. Although linguistically the 'act' and the 'person' may be separated, in real life they rarely are, for the simple reason that the only way we can 'recognize' a person as a person is by interpreting his acts. Even if we start by being speculative in our thinking this is only because, to put it simply, we just have not observed enough acts and we know this. Whenever a person acts he is saying something about his identity even if it is only that he is the sort of person who does not normally behave in this way. A deviant identity is a shorthand way of conceptualizing a person who commits and, as far as we know, is likely to go on committing deviant acts. Careful reading of the above quotation from Hargreaves reveals that in fact it contains an encouragement *not* to dissociate acts from persons. If some acts are inconsistent with a person's self conception then clearly there must be others which are consistent with this conception and therefore exemplars of the identity which the labeller and, hopefully, the person considers desirable.

However, like the previous recommendation on rules, this prescription also contains a useful insight. Clearly, before the labeller can be in a position to persuade the perpetrator that a certain act is 'out of character', he has to arrive at some understanding of what the self concept of the person actually is and what both he and the perpetrator would like it to be. In practice this means the person who commits deviant acts must be communicated with and allowed to express his own views rather than be peremptorily dismissed as a deviant. It allows for a person having a confused identity — a mixture of deviant and conformist elements. It also implies that this examination of the pupil's subjectivity and deviant act is unlikely to be value-free.

The main point being made here is that in-service training based on interactionist concepts does not imply that the EP's traditional contribution of attempting to make education more child-centred has to be abandoned. The difference from previous approaches lies in the emphasis on the importance of an awareness of the social basis of the child's self conception and the general outlook of which it is a part. In interactionist terms a child's view of himself may consist of a constellation of socially generated meanings. Different teachers may think different things about him. He may have a different identity among peers from the one he has at home. Some children are confused about their identity, others are not confused so much as unaware of alternative identities even within their own culture; for instance, the anti-school working-class child who does not appreciate that in another geographical location and in another school it is not considered cissyish to be pro-academic. Knowledge of what alternative self conceptions are available is crucial for helping the child with an identity problem. Teachers also need to consider why children choose one identity rather than another and why some internalize official labels while others reject them.

Curriculum evaluation

The EP's traditional concern with assessment and evaluation can also be construed within an interactionist perspective. An alternative to the traditional modes of curriculum evaluation, for example, is the so-called 'illuminative' approach which is usually theoretically informed by the interactionist perspective. This is a method of evaluation which 'takes account of the wider contexts in which education programmes function' (Hamilton and Parlett, 1972 p. 8). Its primary concern is with description and interpretation rather than measurement and prediction. In relation to the evaluation of a curriculum innovation the aims are:

(a) to study the new programme — how it operates, how it is influenced by the various school situations in which it is applied; what those directly concerned regard as its advantages and disadvantages and how students' intellectual tasks and academic experience are most affected.
(b) to discover and document what it is like to be participating in the scheme, whether as teacher or pupil; and, in addition, to discern and discuss the innovation's most significant features; recurring concomitants and critical processes.

It is clear that a different background knowledge is involved here than can be derived from psychometrics or behavioural psychology. Although this approach does not rule out criterion referenced testing or behavioural objectives analysis, the emphasis is on appreciating the innovation as a social process in a particular context. Finding out how pupils, for example, view the innovation and analysing their ongoing interpretations is an aspect of the evaluation which an interactionist would regard as essential. It would involve more than just asking pupils what they thought of the new project. Although this might be a useful starting point, their responses would need to be interpreted with reference to an understanding of the 'pupil experience' of school. Interactionist studies have thrown light on the variety of strategies that pupils use to get through the school day (see Hammersley and Woods, 1976; Woods, 1980). It might emerge, for example, that the reasons for pupils liking or not liking a curriculum innovation depend more on factors like how disruptive it is of peer group interaction than on the nature of the curriculum material or the teaching method *per se.*

Generally, a major function of the school-based EP is to 'give away' interactionist, social psychology. He will not do himself out of a job until every teacher understands the implications of this perspective. Just as the psychology of the traditional paradigm was used to legitimate certain school practices, so interactionism can be used to reinforce and provide a rationale for those practices consonant with this perspective, such as mixed ability teaching, integration of 'handicapped' pupils, and an 'appreciative' teaching style.

THE CONTEXT OF CHANGE: SOME 'MACRO' CONSIDERATIONS

Appealing though the interactionist perspective may be to the change oriented EP, it does leave some important questions unanswered. Although it provides an interesting description of labelling processes it does not explain why certain types of labelling should be stigmatizing in the first instance. Stigmatization may just be a typical feature of a 'phase' the education system went through, one where psychometrically and medically oriented explanations were relatively dominant. On the other hand it is possible that the 'forces' which produce the stigmatization effect are such an intrinsic feature of the society in which we live that they continue to be influential even with the demise of the traditional paradigm.

It seems to me that the latter view is more consonant with the experiences of EPs. Despite the careful way in which labels are chosen, defined and applied, it usually happens that after a while they become euphemisms for what everybody knows to be derogatory terms, or terms which limit the horizons of the persons to whom they become attached and lower the expectations of those who teach them. For example, what seemed in 1944 to be the successful resolution of the definitional problem in relation to the educationally backward and the psychologically 'disturbed' turns out, over thirty years later, not to have had such beneficial consequences, after all. In 1978, Warnock had this to say about the 'enlightened' descriptive and neutral labels introduced at that time: '... labels tend to stick and children diagnosed as ESN(M) or maladjusted can be stigmatized unnecessarily for the whole of their school careers and beyond' (para. 3.23).

The *déjà vu* experience with respect to the fate of labels and the labelled is common among EPs. What appears to be an innovation based on a new way of looking at problems is eventually perceived for what it is: a gloss on old practices. The intervention designed to help the needy turns out to be counter-productive. Underneath the latest rhetoric and jargon, the dominant ideas in school continue to be those of a previous era. 'Within child' explanations utilizing traditional concepts like ability, capacity, deprivation, disturbance and abnormal retain their popularity among teachers. Basically the old structures of thought and practice remain intact.

At the risk of oversimplifying the sociological issues involved we can conceptualize this lack of real change in two ways — first by referring to cultural underpinnings, and second by drawing on a more radical interpretation of the 'open systems' approach.

To begin with, lack of change may be partially accounted for by the fact that ways of seeing 'disabilities' are embedded 'deep' in the general culture of our society. Many of these attitudes are reflected in ordinary speech and language. We frequently speak of normal being 'good' and abnormal as 'bad'. Shearer (1981) gives many examples of these moral judgements of physical disabilities. Disability is 'evil', we say we have a 'bad' leg or that something is 'wrong' with us. It is a judgement for wrongdoing — the sins of the father. There are many biblical references to disability being unclean and to people with disabilities 'polluting' the normal. Even though many of these associations reflect attitudes of a byegone age, according to Shearer, 'old perceptions cast their shadows still' even in relation to some of the more progressive and enlightened practices.

Second, labels continue to have the same meaning because they reflect 'typifications' which are resistant to change because, for those who hold them, they relate to the reality of school life. Thus, they are embedded in the patterns of social activity which go to make up what we describe as the school system. This system has to articulate with systems outside it and what goes on in schools is therefore partly a function of what happens in the wider society. It is this dimension of change which the EP has traditionally ignored partly because of the influence of positivist and individualist doctrines, but partly also because of others' expectations that he will work at the 'micro' rather than the 'macro' level.

I am suggesting here that if the EP is serious about change then he must situate his practice in the context of an interpretation of the 'world' which includes both micro and macro features. Not to do so would be to fall into the same trap as so many of his predecessors. Either he deludes himself about changes which he imagines to have taken place, or he falls from idealist heights on to the stony ground of pessimism and cynicism.

Conceptions of change vary according to one's model of society at the 'macro' level. By 'macro' I mean the overall pattern of interrelationships characteristic of society. There are two such models which typically underpin conceptions of change in psychological practice — the 'order' and the 'conflict' models of society.

Change within the traditional paradigm tended to be interpreted against the background of an order model. As I suggested earlier in this chapter, this is also the model in the background of practice based on a 'systems' approach. In this model it is assumed that members share an interest in maintaining the basic structures of a system because there is a broad consensus on the cultural values which these structures support. When the system is running smoothly, individuals internalize norms and rules of behaviour which regulate their behaviour in accordance with the overall goals of the system. However, 'strain' can be produced in the system by various sectors being out of phase. For example, there may be a disjuncture between cultural values and the structural arrangements, so that for people located at certain points in the structure goals aspired to go beyond the available means of achieving them. Such strains have to be resolved and the society returned to equilibrium. Traditional and 'systems engineer' EPs sometimes explicitly, but more often implicitly, help to resolve such strain in addition to their wider role of contributing to socialization in 'normal' times.

A major criticism of the order model is that it relies on the questionable assumption that when society is in a state of equilibrium, the interests of all members are being met since they share similar values and aspirations. However, in our society this may be an unwarranted assumption. It could be argued that, even in a state of equilibrium, it is always the case that some groups are achieving their goals while others are not. Moreover, some group's achievements are obtained at the expense of other groups without whose exploitation and acquiescence such success would be impossible. The 'stability' thus attained is the stable situation of one group maintaining its dominance over other groups. Such stability is not in the interests of the subordinate groups who should not therefore have any reason to help maintain the system.

An arguably more realistic model is therefore one which assumes a conflict of interests between groups or classes in society. The notion of a class-divided society implies that for change to be significant it must lead to an alteration in the relationship between classes.

These different approaches to the study of society create different ways of viewing the role of the traditional EP. In terms of the order model, he may attempt to resolve strain by, for example, introducing compensatory education programmes for the educationally disadvantaged who, because of their structural position, do not have an equal opportunity to succeed in the system. Alternatively, compensatory education can be viewed as an ideological construct designed to mask the real function of schooling by diverting attention from the gross inequalities that pervade the whole system at every level and, more importantly perhaps, by not recognizing the role of education in maintaining the acquiescence of the subordinate classes. The egalitarian rhetoric conceals the system-maintaining nature of the exercise. The traditional EP may therefore be construed as colluding with and helping to maintain a system which is not ultimately in the best interests of the majority of children or their parents.

The order model which forms the sociological backcloth of the work of many traditional EPs is not therefore 'neutral' in a political sense. Such a model, sometimes also referred to as a consensus or structural-functionalist model, is consistent with what might be described as a liberal 'world view'. Social problems are conceived in terms which can be dealt with in a reformist, piecemeal fashion without the need for radical changes in existing economic and social structures. Problems are seen as special cases of need creating strain in a system the survival of which is assumed to be necessary.

The liberal view takes for granted the impartial nature of the education system and attempts to define problems in non-political and non-ideological terms. According to George and Wilding (1976) the liberal perspective on social policy is that it is a 'functional accompaniment of industrialisation ... changes in the industrial system upset the equilibrium prevailing among the various parts of the social and economic system with the result that the social policy measures become necessary to restore stability and balance' (p. 7). A class conflict perspective would suggest that there is nothing 'inevitable', in the structural-functionalist sense, about the development of social policy and that the consequences of conceiving social policy in the liberal way are not 'neutral'.

In schools, traditional EPs typically align themselves with liberal ideology. Grace (1978) refers to the several forms which such liberalism can take, but what they all have in common is a piecemeal reformist approach to change. Basically, the traditional EP works within a system which he tacitly supports in actions if not always in words. He helps to legitimate certain educational practices which are not in the best interests of children since they are an aspect of social control which enables the powers that be to maintain their dominance. It is the 'hidden curriculum' of schooling which these EPs largely ignore. The deschooling critique is accepted only in so far as it points the way to manageable reforms, e.g., a change in teachers' attitudes and classroom organization, but is rejected as iconaclistic in its more radical forms. EPs might agree that many schools make children docile (Jules Henry, 1955); encourage the wrong sort of learner behaviour (Holt, 1964 and Bruner, 1966); are imbued with competitiveness (Hargreaves, 1972); are not child-centred enough, too exam oriented, etc; but there is no sense of the profound alienation of schools which stunts the growth and reduces the potential of most children (see Holly, 1972). This oppressive role of schools is masked by a definition of individual needs and potential which is limited to what is known or what is thought possible from evidence derived from knowledge of children's functioning in a class society where, by definition, the majority of children's intellectual, emotional and social functioning is depressed. A less restricted definition of need and potential would require the recognition of such widespread underfunctioning that only radical changes in the social and economic structure and a complete reorientation of values and priorities could produce a situation where the educational needs of all children were genuinely met. Traditional EPs help to provide the system with credibility by providing a definition of educational need which is manageable or at least potentially manageable within the system. Their definitions based on their 'science' are likely to be manageable because they derive, in the final analysis, from the dominant values of the social order which are also incorporated in the education system.

THE EDUCATIONAL PSYCHOLOGIST AS A RADICAL CHANGE AGENT

For many change-oriented EPs, particularly those who favour the interactionist perspective, the liberal view of schools based on an order model of society is unacceptable. Their experience of working with the problems of the system leads them to think more in terms of radical options than piecemeal reform. As previously suggested, many of them have experienced *déjà vu* with respect to the tenacity of deviant labelling processes, and the lack of basic change in the system is blatantly obvious to them. Such EPs opt for the alternative perspective of radical change based on a recognition of the profound alienation in schools and a conflict rather than an order model of society.

This is not to suggest that the radical is unconcerned with reforms, but support for reforms takes place in the context of a radical critique of schools and schooling. Like Young (1979) it might be useful to conceive of reforms as not without contradictions:

'Reforms, because they emerge from a class divided society, will always display such a two-sided nature. The search then for the 'pure reform' is a chimera which we can well do without' (p. 27).

Although reforms have to be pressed for, it is important for the radical to adopt a certain attitude towards them and to see them as part of an overall strategy. As Statham (1978) points out:

> The necessity is to keep pressing for change and movement in a way which resists categorization as the solution to the problem but at the same time to recognize the changes achieved within the existing socio-economic structure will be profoundly inadequate. (p. 71)

OUTLINES FOR A RADICAL PRACTICE

With the above in mind I want to conclude by suggesting some outlines for a radical practice. In so doing I shall draw on the work of Cohen (1975) who, although writing for social workers, has raised issues which are relevant to radical practice in all professions.

The role of theory

According to Cohen practitioners should tell theoreticians who urge them to be more theoretically sophisticated to get off their backs! This is worth mentioning because it probably does not apply to radical EPs. In fact the opposite, if anything, should really be suggested. All EPs, radicals included, need to be more concerned with theory. In the past there has been an overemphasis on practice to the virtual exclusion of theory (see Quicke, 1977). EPs have in C. Wright Mills' (1942) term become 'paste-pot' eclectics who derive their practices from an eclecticism 'that does not analyse in an adequate way the elements and theories which it seeks to combine' (p. 169). We can see this in relation to most of the practices which have sought to move away from the traditional paradigm, particularly the behavioural approach which is an odd mixture of behaviourism, humanistic psychology and child development models against a functionalist sociological backcloth. As the chapter on that approach suggested, there was no adequate theoretical analysis of the various elements.

Cohen's point is probably more true for social workers because of the significance of sociological theory in their training. An introduction to various theoretical positions and the politics of these is more a feature of social work training than EP training.

Psychology is the dominant theoretical component of EP training and this, as I have indicated, is itself dominated by a positivist view which underplays the role of theory and inhibits theoretical discussion particularly in the cognate areas of sociology and philosophy.

The radical change agent EP should, therefore, be more theoretically sophisticated, but this is not to say that he should adopt a 'purist' approach. Some form of eclecticism is probably inevitable because of the partial nature of most theories, but the EP should be aware of the possible contradictions involved in using 'bits and pieces' from various theories and he should certainly analyse these 'in an adequate way' and struggle for consistency in both theory and practice.

The ideology of case work

Cohen recommends that radicals refuse the 'ideology' of case work but nevertheless still think of cases. This suggestion is relevant for radical EPs because it addresses the dilemma referred to previously in the discussion on working on a non-referral basis. Again, the situation is rather different from that of social workers. Unlike social workers, EPs are not legally obliged to take action in relation to individual clients, although they are often under strong pressure to do so, particularly in the current period. It is still possible for EPs to see very few children individually to an extent that would be impossible for a social worker. Reducing the number of individuals seen on a formal basis, therefore, is a realistic option for EPs.

However, in so far as the EP does have contact with and make recommendations about individual children or groups of children whom he has seen on a non-referral basis he can 'refuse the ideology of casework' by going even further than Cohen and not treating them as 'cases' in any sense.

At the same time, of course, one does attempt to work with organizations as well as with individual clients. In the case of the radical social worker, as Cohen points out, the constituency will be claimant's unions, tenant's associations, etc. The radical EP should relate to forces inside schools, and organizations and pressure groups both inside and outside school, official and unofficial. His strategy for changing the system may be to develop counter-systems (see Leonard, 1975). It is not an easy matter to ascertain which organizations or groups do actually function as counter-systems, i.e., as systems opposed to the dominant ideology and structure. In the case of schools, it could be a small radically-oriented group of teachers within a school or, if radical ideas have widespread support among the staff, including the headteacher, it could be the whole school. As far as groups and organizations outside school are concerned much depends on the idiosyncracies of the locality. In some areas, for example, there are a number of 'community groups' which are sufficiently active and well established to be a significant force for change. I am thinking particularly of those groups which emerge to fill a political vaccum in the 'welfare' area. Groups of most relevance for radical EPs would be those associated with, say, nursery provision or mental health. Other organizations, like trade unions, which have evolved from the collective self activity of the historically oppressed majority in society, should also be considered as useful allies.

Deviant labelling

Cohen's third point is that the insights of deviancy theory should be taken seriously. 'Think very concretely about how to avoid stigmatizing your clients, unwittingly facilitating their drift in to further troubles, trapping them in cycles of rejection' (p. 95). I have already discussed some of the implications of the interactionist perspective for psychological practice in schools, and in discussing Cohen's second suggestion have advocated abandoning the case work model. However, in the present circumstances, it is unlikely that the EP will be able to avoid seeing at least some individuals as 'cases' in relation to SE procedures. When he does, he needs to continually remind himself at every stage of the procedure of the dangers of deviant labelling.

One solution to this problem has been for EPs to co-operate so far with SE procedures by accepting referrals and assessing individual children, but then adopting a policy of rarely recommending a special school or class placement. There are a number of practical difficulties with this approach. For example, schools are often alienated by this persistent refusal of EPs to make such a recommendation. Many teachers are quite genuine in their feeling that all parties are likely to benefit from a special school placement. The child benefits by receiving extra attention and specialist help in a more sympathetic environment, 'normal' children benefit because more teacher time can be devoted to them and the teacher benefits because she can spend more time on 'educational' rather than 'managerial/disciplinary' activities. It is difficult for the EP not to have some sympathy with these views, particularly if he is attempting to be appreciative of the teacher role. Yet the contradictions involved are clear. It is not only the small number of children who are sent to special schools who are at risk of being stigmatized. The process of selecting these few candidates cannot actually be carried out without involving many more children in vast screening and diagnostic 'sweeps' of school populations. Such 'sweeps' tend to throw up many more children who, while not suitable for a special school, clearly require some form of special help in the way this has been traditionally defined, i.e., with the risk of deviant labelling. Moreover, the notion of a substantial minority of children with special educational needs as opposed to a majority with 'normal' needs is continually being legitimized and reinforced. In short, if you have special schools you usually cannot avoid the development of an extensive SE apparatus which has implications for the education system as a whole.

Demystifying traditional practice

One aspect of unmasking 'pretensions and euphemisms', as Cohen advises, is to develop an ongoing critique in schools and school psychological services of explanations of conduct which are influenced by 'scientific' psychology.

The radical EP may find himself in a minority position among his colleagues over such issues as intelligence testing and special education. Some other EPs are likely to regard his views on these issues as too extreme, yet in fact they are often only a logical extension of their own views. For example, many EPs do not support radical policies to dismantle the SE apparatus, but say they are against 'labelling'. Also, many EPs recognize the 'scientistic' nature of intelligence tests and yet will reach for a test in order to produce 'hard data' in support of a recommendation when this is likely to be queried by other professionals or the administration.

Demystification should involve confronting the traditional paradigm with an imputation of what it claims not to be: an ideology. It is important to remember that even the alleged alternatives to that paradigm also claim to be 'scientific' and valuefree. Behavioural psychology, for example, like psychometrics, is a classic instance of an attempt to mystify by claiming scientific status. London (1972) regarded the behaviour modification movement as an example of the 'end of ideology' thesis (see Bell, 1960) in action. He distinguished between 'theory' (scientific) and 'ideology' (not scientific). The latter is more to do with polemics, and acts as a basis for commitment and a 'rallying point' for practitioners. He considered that debates between practitioners prior to the coming of age of the behaviour modification movement were ideological rather than scientific debates.

There is a tendency for EPs who embrace the behavioural perspective to de-emphasize the value framework within which they are working and to assume that classroom behaviour can be observed in a neutral and objective manner. This leads to a technical and empiricist approach to problem solving which gives low priority to theoretical discussion. The emphasis is on the technology of change rather than theoretical explanation, on the 'facts', the here and now context rather than remote causes. The real issue for London is not whether one theory provides a better explanation than another theory but revolves around the 'consequences of the treatment . . . for the person's condition or his life' (p. 915). Thus the only important question about treatment 'is that of the simultaneous relevance of the treatment technique to the person's manifest trouble and to the rest of his life' (p. 915). Such statements are made as if the problem, i.e., 'trouble', could be defined in a theory-free way.

Demystifying the traditional paradigm is likely to present the EP with professional 'survival' problems since so much of his identity is bound up with the 'scientist' image. Indeed the fact that this paradigm has reflected the interests of EPs is one of the main features of its nature as an ideology. Schools have tended to be mystified by talk of special difficulties and problems which have been diagnosed by using specialist psychological techniques and require special treatment. Neither behaviouralism nor the nondirective style resolves this problem adequately because, as we have seen, both in fact rely on expertise from the traditional paradigm.

Staying 'unfinished'

According to Cohen (drawing on the work of Mathiesen, 1974) staying unfinished means becoming involved in short-term, humanitarian reforms without losing sight of long-term goals. His analysis provides an insight into the thorny problem of which reforms are most appropriate from a radical perspective. He recommends that the 'points of departure' should be those reforms which are closest to the clients' needs as they perceive them in and here and now, but although one should work 'at what is close at hand' this should always be in the 'direction of abolition'.

In addition to the traditional paradigm, at a more concrete level, the mere existence of special schools and SE structures provides a status quo maintaining framework for the education system and therefore the radical would do well to think in terms of how best to abolish them. Unlike Cohen, however, I am not suggesting that one merely aims for abolition and actually resists 'the pressure to make positive reforms'. It seems to me that if in the process of abolition the opportunity for an obvious and readily implemented reform reveals itself then it should be seized. Indeed, if one is also concerned with reforms that are close to clients, why should it not be?

In relation to special schools, as indicated in the section on deviant labelling, there are certain tactical problems raised by a unilateral opting out from involvement in special education. The apparent lack of appreciation of the teacher role may result in a loss of credibility in the short term.

A useful compromise here which might be acceptable to radicals is to retain a foothold in SE at the same time as working for changes in the way special schools are conceived. That is rather than, say, attempting to improve special schools so that they carry out the function for which they were designed (i.e.,the traditional approach), the radical should attempt to obtain a consensus about the need to change special schools into experimental or alternative schools. Such schools would provide a variety of experimental regimes to cater for the needs of any child who was referred to them. Attendance would be voluntary and all children should be eligible. There would be no criteria of handicap or special need involved and therefore no need for formal ascertainment under the appropriate section of the 1944 Act or for screening surveys. The procedures for entry would be entirely informal and would depend on negotiations between the head and the referring agency, e.g., a parent, a teacher, an EP, or the child himself. These schools might contain a mixture of children, some of whom previously might have been categorized as special and others who were making 'normal' progress in school, but who for one reason or another wanted a break from traditional schooling. The relationship between the experimental and the neighbouring schools would depend on a number of factors, but the ideal situation would be for the former to act as an example to the latter of the best progressive practices. In fact, the experimental school should attempt to turn itself into a base whence progressive and radical teachers and EPs, who would be closely involved with such schools, could make forays into the ordinary school. In addition to links that would develop naturally as a result of teachers visiting ordinary schools to see potential recruits, and to follow up children who opted to return to the mainstream, a system of staff exchanges could be introduced whereby teachers in ordinary and special schools changed places every so often.

It is worth noting that this system would counter the criticism often made of those who oppose special schooling that they are in fact providing ammunition for those whose task it is to cut education services. It should be made clear that just as much plant and equipment and just as many teachers would be needed for an alternative as for a special system of schools.

The demand for this reform seems to be realistic. It is not so far removed from present realities as to be beyond the thinking of most practitioners in this area. Indeed, in many ways, the change from special to alternative could be construed as the end point of many current trends in SE practices. Some authorities operate an informal system of special school placements. In many it is possible for children to spend half their time in the special school and half in the ordinary school (or whatever proportions are appropriate). Schools may be officially labelled ESN or Maladjusted but may take a wide range of children, some of whom have minor, others more serious, difficulties. The reform is also compatible with 'integrationist' thinking.

However, this is not to deny the radical nature of this proposal which is basically founded on the notion that 'all children are special' and denies the possibility of SE acting as an ideological and practical support for the system. The idea of SE is so ingrained in the thinking of planners and policy makers and so important to the rationale of welfare provision in education that it is a 'touch and go' question as to whether or not the system can accommodate the proposals outlined above, modest as they may seem to be.

The democratic attitude

It is implicit in the interactionist approach that one would not 'sell out your clients' interests for the sake of ideological purity or theoretical neatness' (p. 95). Even the most ardent of radicals should recognize the tension between the desire to impose one's own 'correct' definition of the situation and the desire to respect the views of others whose 'worlds' one can never fully understand. The interactionist aims at a negotiative style which involves plunging into the hurly burly of social life in schools. In so doing, he cannot avoid taking account of the power differentials between participants and the effect this has on the outcome of negotiations.

It is in so far as the power differential involves the imposition of definitions which are status quo maintaining that he is opposed to the prevailing power structure and seeks to democratize the institutions within which he works. He can do no better in this respect than to start in his own backyard.

A typical example of the threat to democracy within school psychological services is the increasing tendency towards a hierarchical structure linked with rationalization programmes in the local authority administration. The SPS hierarchy is scarcely an oppressive, authoritarian pecking order. There is usually plenty of negotiation between superiors and subordinates, and a reasonable degree of autonomy for all. But 'little hierarchies' have sprung up. In some areas so-called 'field' EPs (i.e., those who spend most of their time on professional work rather than administration) are increasingly being removed from important decision making areas, particularly when there is an interlocking of hierarchies under a corporate management system.

CONCLUSION

This book has been concerned with the social determinants of educational psychological practice. Various attempts to transcend the limits imposed by the way such practice has been structured have been explored and their faltering nature in the face of prevailing social forms demonstrated. If the emphasis has been on the inevitable failure of changes made without due regard to their meaning in the immediate social psychological setting or to their relationship to the wider social structure, this is because the author is somewhat pessimistic about the prospects for genuine radical change in the present circumstances. The general drift of the thesis, therefore, is in the direction of a portrait of educational psychology as mainly a conservative profession, conforming to a traditional paradigm, overpreoccupied with professional issues and operating in the context of an education system the role of which it does not fully explore.

However, this is to be too fatalistic. This final chapter is intended to redress the balance. The total failure of practice aimed at radical, progressive goals is not inevitable. Radical activity may appear to have little hope of succeeding in the short term, but this is not to say that something is not gained from the experience of such activity. Radical proposals only reinforce disillusionment and frustration if they are carried out in a 'heady' optimistic fashion without due regard for the forces which may prevent their realization.

As for the traditional practitioner paradigm, although a complete break from it has been advocated, this is not to imply that *all* the practices which took place within its parameters can be dismissed as worthless. The radical perspective based on a more thoroughgoing social psychological approach does *not* have any continuities with 'modern educational psychology' in terms of the knowledge base, but many of the educational recommendations which emerged from a grounding in the traditional base do have ideological affinities with what I have described as radical practice. In fact, radical practice takes up some of the traditional concerns such as integration; opposition to the medical model; alternative, progressive, experimental education; child centredness; and reinterprets them in ways which are more vigorously oppositional to the status quo and more faithful, even than the activities of some of the early pioneers, to humanist ideals.

APPENDIX 1

Letter to educational psychologists

The University of Sheffield,
Division of Education,
Floor 9,
Arts Tower,
Sheffield S10 2TN
Tel: Sheffield 78555,
STD code: 0742

JCQ/EN 20th March, 1978

To: the Principal Educational Psychologist

Dear Sir,
    I was wondering if you and your staff (i.e. educational psychologists) would be interested in assisting in some research I am doing into aspects of the educational psychologist's professional knowledge? If so, I should be grateful if you would complete and return the enclosed questionnaires.
    Although the main purpose of the questionnaire is to provide data for a fairly long term research project, the responses will, hopefully, provide information which will be of immediate use in the teaching and training of educational psychologists.
    If you would like to discuss the questionnaire before or after filling it in, please do not hesitate to contact me. The questionnaire has been piloted but even at this stage I would welcome further comments and (wholesale!) criticism.
    If you require more questionnaires could you please inform me and I will send them immediately.

                        Yours sincerely,

                John Quicke, B.A., Dip.Ed.Psych.
                Lecturer in Educational Psychology

APPENDIX 2

The questionnaire on professional knowledge

DIVISION AND INSTITUTE OF EDUCATION

PROFESSIONAL KNOWLEDGE QUESTIONNAIRE

Please Return to: J. C. Quicke, Floor 9, Arts Tower, University, Sheffield

1. Please indicate in the space provided the extent to which you use the following tests, i.e.

   $\sqrt{\sqrt{}}$ = I use this test regularly $\sqrt{}$ = I use this only occasionally.

   0 = I hardly ever use this/I never use this.

   Add other tests to the list if you wish

   ..... WISC(R)
   ..... WPPSI
   ..... WAIS
   ..... Stanford Binet
   ..... Progressive Matrices
   ..... AH4
   ..... Boehm Test of Basic Concepts
   ..... Goodenough Harris Man Drawing
   ..... Bender Visual Motor Gestalt Test
   ..... Frostig Test of Visual Perception
   ..... English Picture Vocab. Test
   ..... Reynell Developmental Language Scales
   ..... ITPA
   ..... Manchester Scales of Social Adaptation
   ..... Vineland Social Maturity Scale
   ..... Eysenck Personality Inventories (JMPI, JE, etc.)
   ..... Cattell HSPQ (or other)
   ..... Repertory Grid Technique
   ..... Family Relations (Bene Anthony)
   ..... Thematic Appercetion Test
   ..... Columbia Mental Maturity Scale
   .....
   ..... Stott Social Adjustment Guides

The questionnaire on professional knowledge

..... Schonell RI .....
..... Burt Rearranged Graded .....
    Word Reading Test .....
..... Neale Analysis of .....
    Reading Ability .....

2. Will you be using the British Ability Scales? (please tick where appropriate)

..... Almost certainly on a regular basis   ..... Possibly only occasionally
..... Possibly on a regular basis   ..... I shall rarely use the BAS
..... Almost certainly only occasionally   ..... I shall not be using the BAS at all.

3. If you do not use psychometric tests please indicate, as briefly as possible, your main reasons.

4. Please indicate your preferences in relation to the following perspectives in psychology, i.e.

   $\sqrt{\sqrt{}}$ = strongly prefer $\sqrt{}$ = weakly prefer
   0 = have no particular view on   X = have a negative attitude towards

   Add other perspectives if you wish

   ..... Behaviourist   ..... Humanistic
   ..... Psychoanalytic   ..... Experimental
   ..... Psychometric   ..... Developmental
   ..... Phenomenological   ..... Symbolic Interactionist
   ..... Cognitive   ..... Information-processing
   ..... Positivist   .....
   ..... Historical Materialist .....
   ..... Sociologically Oriented .....
   ..... Eclectic   .....

5. Please indicate if you have consciously and deliberately drawn on the work of any of these psychologists as a resource in your day to day practice.

   $\sqrt{\sqrt{}}$ = regularly $\sqrt{}$ = occasionally 0 = hardly ever X = never

   Add other psychologists if you wish

   ..... S. Freud   ..... R. B. Cattell   ..... W. Reich
   ..... J. Piaget   ..... G. W. Allport   ..... R. Harre
   ..... J. S. Bruner   ..... J. Bowlby   ..... C. G. Jung
   ..... C. Burt   ..... M. Rutter   ..... A. Adler

154 / *The Cautious Expert*

.....L. S. Vygotsky	.....A. Maslow	.....C. L. Hull
.....C. Rogers	.....P. E. Vernon	.....A. R. Jensen
.....G. Kelly	.....D. H. Stott	.....D. P. Ausubel
.....B. F. Skinner	.....R. Laing	.....J. B. Watson
.....H. J. Eysenck	.....G. H. Mead	.....J. Wolpe
.....E. Fromm	.....R. M. Gagne	.....
.....M. Argyle	.....H. Marcuse	.....
.....B. S. Bloom	.....E. Goffman	.....

6. Please indicate if you have consciously and deliberately drawn on the work of any of these educationists as a resource in your day to day practice.

   √√ = regularly √ = occasionally 0 = hardly ever X = never

   Add to the list if you wish

.....B. Bernstein	.....D. Holly	.....J. Henry	.....
.....C. B. Cox	.....G. H. Bantock	.....J. Dewey	.....
.....H. Holt	.....I. R. Dale	.....J. Vaizey	.....
.....A. H. Halsey	.....D. Hamilton	.....P. H. Hirst	.....
.....A. E. Dyson	.....G. Esland	.....R. Williams	.....
.....B. Simon	.....L. Stenhouse	.....H. Gintis	.....
.....R. S. Peters	.....M. F. D. Young	.....I. Illich	.....
.....J. B. Nisbet	.....W. Labov	.....D. Hargreaves	.....
.....D. F. Swift	.....N. J. Entwistle	.....B. Jackson	.....
.....A. Cicourel	.....P. Freire	.....A. E. Tansley	.....

7. Name any books and/or articles on education, psychology or related disciplines which you have read in the past year and which have made a significant impact on your professional practice.

8. How often do you consult the following journals?

   √√ = regularly √ = occasionally 0 = hardly ever/not at all

   Add to the list if you wish

.....British Journal of Educ. Psychol.	.....British Journal of Psychology
.....Journal of Child Psychol. Psychiatry	.....Special Education
.....Remedial Education	.....Theraputic Education
.....British Journal of Guidance and Counselling	.....Radical Education
.....The Teacher	.....
.....Rank and File	.....
.....Hard Cheese	.....
.....Times Educational Supplement	.....
.....AEP Journal	.....

The questionnaire on professional knowledge / 155

..... British Journal of Sociology   .....
..... Bulletin of the BPS   .....
..... Humpty Dumpty   .....
..... Child Development   .....
..... Educational Research   .....
..... Harvard Educational Review   .....
..... New Society   .....

9. Are you optimistic that future research in psychology will produce findings which will make a positive and significant contribution towards solving some of the more persistent educational problems?

10. Which professional organisation(s) do you belong to (e.g., AEP, BPS)?

11. (optional) Name: ....

    Service:. ....

12. Additional comments

APPENDIX 3

Questionnaire results

Rank order list derived from results of questionnaire study.

1. *Tests*
a) For *regular* use

		% (rounded)
1.	Wechsler Intelligence Scale for Children	82
2.	Neale Analysis of Reading Ability	52
3.	Stanford-Binet	42
4.	Burt Rearranged Graded Word Reading Test	36
5.	Bender Visual Motor Gestalt Test	31
6.	English Picture Vocabulary Test	29
7.	Wechsler Pre-School and Primary Scale of Intelligence	29
8.	Goodenough Harris Man Drawing	24
9.	Bristol Social Adjustment Guides	23
10.	Reynell Developmental Lanuage Scales	21
11.	Schonell RI	20
12.	Eysenck Personality Inventories	12
13.	Illinois Test of Psycholinguistic Abilities	11
14.	Repertory Grid Technique	11
15.	Bene Anthony Family Relations Test	11
16.	Vineland Social Maturity Scale	10
17.	Progressive Matrices	10
18.*	Merrill Palmer Pre-School Performance	7
19.	Frostig Test of Visual Perception	6
	Rest below	5

b) For *combined* usage, i.e., regular *plus* occasional users, the following figures were obtained:

		%
1.	The Wechsler Intelligence Scale for Children	94

* The Merril Palmer was the only test added by respondents which was above the 5% mark for regular use.

2.	Neale Analysis of Reading Ability	84
3.	Stanford-Binet	81
4.	English Picture Vocabulary Test	79
5.	Reynell Developmental Language Scales	74
6.	Wechsler Pre-School and Primary Scales of Intelligence	73
7.	Bender Visual Motor Gestalt Test	71
8.	Goodenough Harris Man Drawing	71
9.	Burt Rearranged Graded Word Reading Test	71
10.	Vineland Social Maturity Scale	67
11.	Illinois Test of Psycholinguistic Abilities	67
12.	Bristol Social Adjustment Guides	62
13.	Bene Anthony Family Relations Test	62
14.	Frostig Test of Visual Perception	56
15.	Progressive Matrices	46
16.	Wechsler Adult Intelligence Scales	45
17.	Schonell RI	45
18.	Repertory Grid Technique	44
19.	Eysenck Personality Inventories	44
20.	Cattell	30
21.	Thematic Apperception Test	29
22.	Columbia Mental Maturity Scale	26
23.	Manchester Scales of Social Adaptation	19
24.	Boehm Test of Basic Concepts	17
25.	Merrill Palmer Pre-School Performance	14
26.	AH4	11

2. Perspectives
a) For *strongly preferred*

	% rounded			%
1. Eclectic	49	8. Phenomenological		9
2. Developmental	39	9. Sociological		6
3. Behaviourist	36	10. Information Processing		6
4. Psychometric	17	11. Psychoanalysis		5
5. Cognitive	15	12. Symbolic Interactionism		7
6. Experimental	14	13. Historical	⎫	less than 5 (also
7. Humanistic	10	Materialism	⎬	those added by
		14. Positivism	⎭	respondents)

b) For 'strong' and 'weak' *combined* (the other categories 'have no particular view on' and 'have a negative attitude towards')

	%		%
1. Developmental	86	8. Psychoanalytic	40
2. Behaviourist	76	9. Humanistic	37
3. Eclectic	74	10. Information Processing	30
4. Psychometric	65	11. Phenomenological	29
5. Cognitive	62	12. Symbolic Interactionism	13
6. Experimental	62	13. Positivist	10
7. Sociological	45	14. Hist. Materialist	4

158 / *The Cautious Expert*

3. **Psychologists**
a) *Regular Use*

	% rounded		%
1. B. F. Skinner	31	8. J. S. Bruner	
2. J. Piaget	30	9. S. Freud	11
3. M. Rutter	19	10. H. Eysenck	
4. G. Kelly	18	11. J. Bowlby	10
5. D. H. Stott	16	12. J. Wolpe	9
6. C. Rogers	15	13. P. E. Vernon	8
7. C. Burt	13	14. M. Argyle	8
		15. R. B. Cattell	5
		The Rest below	5
		(including those added by respondents)	

b) *Combined Use* (use regularly or occasionally)

	%		%
1. J. Piaget	88	16. R. D. Laing	37
2. M. Rutter	76	17. J. Wolpe	34
3. B, F. Skinner	72	18. J. B. Watson	31
4. D. H. Stott	71	19. C. L. Hull	24
5. C. Rogers	66	20. C. G. Jung	24
6. J. Bowlby	59	21. G. Allport	24
7. C. Burt	59	22. A. Maslow	21
8. G. Kelly	59	23. A. Jensen	21
9. J. S. Bruner	58	24. R. M. Gagne	19
10. H. Eysenck	54	25. E. Goffman	16
11. S. Freud	53	26. E. Fromm	15
12. P. Vernon	50	27. B. S. Bloom	15
13. M. Argyle		28. A. Adler	
14. L. S. Vygotsky	45	29. D. P. Ausubel	14
15. R. B. Cattell	40	30. G. Mead	11
		The Rest below	10
		(including additions)	

4. **Educationists**
a) *Regular Use*

	% rounded
1. A. E. Tansley	16
2. B. Bernstein	10
3. D. Hargreaves	8
4. J. Holt	5
The Rest below	5

b) *Combined use* (regular or occasional)

	%		%
1. A. E. Tansley	67	9. N. J. Entwistle	18
2. B. Bernstein	64	10. J. Dewey	15
3. D. Hargreaves	32	11. M. F. D. Young	12
4. J. Holt	30	12. W. Labov	10
5. R. S. Peters	25	13. J. B. Nisbet	

Questionnaire results / 159

6. A. H. Halsey	25		14. J. Vaizey		8
7. I. Illich	} 23		15. B. Simon		7
8. B. Jackson			The Rest	below	5

5. *Reading*
a) *Regular Consultation*

		%
1.	*Journal of the Association of Educational Psychologists*	62
2.	*British Psychological Society Bulletin*	57
3.	*The Times Educational Supplement*	39
4.	*British Journal of Educational Psychology*	33
5.	*Journal of Child Psychology Psychiatry*	30
6.	*Special Education*	20
7.	*Educational Research*	15
8.	*Remedial Education*	13
9.	*Therapeutic Education*	8
10.	*New Society*	7
11.	*British Journal of Psychology*	4
12.	*Child Development*	3
13.	*The Teacher*	2

b) *Combined (Regular or Occasional)*

		%
1.	*Journal of the Association of Educational Psychologists*	84
2.	*The Times Educational Supplement*	83
3.	*British Psychological Society Bulletin*	83
4.	*British Journal of Educational Psychology*	81
5.	*Journal of Child Psychology Psychiatry*	67
6.	*Special Education*	64
7.	*Educational Research*	62
8.	*Remedial Education*	59
9.	*New Society*	48
10.	*Child Development*	40
11.	*British Journal of Psychology*	32
12.	*Therapeutic Education*	28
13.	*The Teacher*	19
14.	*Harvard Educational Review*	12
15.	*British Journal of Guidance and Counselling*	10
16.	*Humpty Dumpty*	9
17.	*British Journal of Sociology*	8
18.	*Rank and File*	3
19.	*Radical Education*	1
20.	*Hard Cheese*	Less than 1
	The Rest	Less than 1

References

AINSCOW, M, and TWEDDLE, D. (1977) 'Behavioural objectives and children with learning difficulties', AEP *Journal*, Vol. 4, no. 5, pp. 29—33.

ALEXANDER, Sir W. (1964) 'Week by week', Column in *Education*, 8 May 1964.

BANKS, C. (1953) 'Symposium on psychologists and psychiatrists in Child Guidance Services, VI — research in child guidance', *British Journal of Educational Psychology*, Voo. XXIII, Feb. pp. 1—7.

BANNON, W. J. (1965) 'From the Presidential Chair', AEP *Newsletter*, No. 4, Autumn.

BECKER, W. C. et al. (1967) 'The contingent use of teacher attention and praise in reducing classroom problems', *Journal of Special Education*, pp. 287—307.

BELL, D. (1960) *The End of Ideology*, Free Press.

BERGER, P. L. and LUCKMANN, T. (1967) *The Social Construction of Reality*, Penguin.

BERSOFF, D. N. (1973) 'Silk purses into sow's ears. The decline of psychological testing and a suggestion for its redemption', *American Psychologist* 28, pp. 892—9.

BITENSKY, R. (1973) 'The influence of political power in determining the theoretical development of social work', *Journal of Social Policy* 2, pp. 119—30.

BLACKHAM, G. J. and SILBERMAN, A. (1971) *Modification of Child Behaviour*, Wadsworth.

BLUMER, H. (1969) *Symbolic Interactionism*, Englewood Cliffs, N.J., Prentice Hall.

Board of Education (1938) *Report of the Committee of Inquiry into Problems Relating to Children with Defective Hearing*, London, HMSO.

Board of Education (1934) *Report of the Committee of Inquiry into Problems Relating to Partially Sighted Children*, London, HMSO.

BOOTH, TONY, (1981) 'Demystifying integration' in *The Practice of Special Education*, Basil Blackwell in association with the Open University Press.

BRUNER, J. S. (1966) *Toward a Theory of Instruction*, Norton.

BULLOCK, A. (1975) *A Language for Life*, HMSO.

BURDEN, R. (1981) 'Systems theory and its relevance to schools', in GILLMAN, B. *Problem Behaviour in the Secondary School*, Croom Helm.

BURNS, R. G. and RUPIPER, O. J. (1977) 'Trends in School Psychology', *Psychology in The Schools*, Vol. XIV, No. 3, pp. 332—340.

BURT, C. (1953) 'Symposium on psychologists and psychiatrists in the Child Guidance Service VII — Conclusion', *British Journal of Educational Psychology*, Vol. 23, pp. 8—27.

BURT, C. (1979) 'The concept of intelligenge', AEP *Journal and Newsletter*, Vol. 2, No. 5, Spring, pp. 16—38.

CASHDAN, A. (1969) 'Handicaps in Learning', in MORRIS, J. F. and LUNZER, E. A. *Development in Learning: Centexts of Education*, London, Staple Press.

CHAZAN, M., MOORE, T., WILLIAMS, P. and WRIGHT, J. (1974) *The Practice of Educational Psychology*, Longman.

COHEN, S. (1975) 'It's all right for you to talk: political and sociological manifestos for social work action', in BAILEY, R. and BRAKE, M. *Radical Social Work*, Edward Arnold.

COOKE, C. T. (1977) 'The practice of educational psychology: an obscure Profession', *Psychology Teaching*, Vol. 5, No. 2, Nov., pp. 158—161.

Court Report (*Fit for the Future*), *The Report of the Committee on Child Health Services*, cmnd. 6684. (1976) HMSO.

CRABTREE, T. W. (1968) in the *Journal and Newletter* of the AEP, Vol. 2, No. 3, p. 24.

CRONBACH, L. J. (1971) 'Test Validation' in THORNDIKE, R. L. (Ed.) *Educational Measurement*, (2nd ed.), Washington, D.C., American Council on Education.

DALE, R. (1972) *The Culture of the School*, The Open University Press.

DALE, R. (1977) *Liberal and Radical Alternatives*, The Open University Press.

DAVIDSON, M. (1952), Symposium on psychologists and psychiatrists in Child Guidance Services, No. II, *British Journal of Educational Psychology*, Vol. 22, pp. 1—4.

DENT, H. C. (1977) *The Training of Teachers in England and Wales*, Hodder and Stoughton.

Department of Education and Science, Circular 3/74; DHSS Circular HSC(15)9; Welsh Office Circular WHSC(15)5, Child Guidance (14th March 1974).

DES Circular 2/75, Welsh Office 21/75, *The Discovery of Children Requiring Special Education and the Assessment of their Needs*, 17 March 1975.

DESSENT, T. (1976) Some alternative approaches in educational psychology: an interview study, M.A. Thesis, University of Nottingham.

Division of Educational and Child Psychology (DECP) (1978) Psychological services for children, *Bulletin of the British Psychological Society*, Vol. 31, pp. 11—15.

DECP. British Psychological Society, Northern Branch Meeting, (20 March 1976) 'Account of discussion of Hargreaves' Paper — the deviant pupil in the secondary school'.

DONALDSON, M. (1978) *Children's Minds*, Fontana.

ELLIOT, C. (1974) 'Intelligence and the British Intelligence Scale', *Bulletin of the British Psychological Society*, Vol. 27, pp. 313—17.

ELLIOT, C. (1975) 'Innovation and decision-making in psychological assessment', Paper presented to the Annual Conference of the British Psycological Society.

ELLIOT, P. (1973) 'Professional Ideology and Social Science', *Sociological Review*, Vol. 21, No. 2, May, pp. 211—28.

ENTWISTLE, H. (1970) *Child-Centred Education*, Methuen.

ENTWISTLE, H. (1978) *Class, Culture and Education*, Methuen.

FREEMAN, A. G. and TOPPING, K. J. (1976) 'What do you expect of an educational psychologist?' AEP *Journal*, Vol. 4, No. 3, pp. 4—9.

GALLOWAY, D. (1981) 'Institutional change or individual change? An overview', in GILLHAM, B, *Problem Behaviour in the Secondary School*, Croom Helm.

GEORGE, V. and WILDING, P. (1976) *Ideology and Social Welfare*, RKP.

GIDDENS, A. (1976) *New Rules of Sociological Method*, Hutchinson.

GILLHAM, W. E. C. (1974) 'The British Intelligence Scale: *à la recherche du temps perdu*', *Bulletin of the British Psychological Society*, Vol. 27, pp. 307—12.

GILLHAM, BILL (1978) *Reconstructing Educational Psychology*, Croom Helm, London.

GOLDSTEIN, H. and BLINKHORN, S. (1977) 'Monitoring educational Standards. An inappropriate model', *Bulletin of the BPS*, Vol. 30, pp. 309—11.

GRACE, G. (1978) *Teachers, Ideology and Control*, RKP.

GRAHAM, C. (1970) 'The relation between ability and attainment tests', in JAMES, C. (ed.) 'Modern concepts of intelligence', AEP *Journal and Newsletter*, Vol. 2, No. 5, Spring.

GREEN, A. (1946) 'Social Values and Psychotherapy', *Journal of Personality*.

GUNTRIP, H. (1968) *Schizoid Phenomena, Object-Relations and the Self*, London, Hogarth Press.

HAMILTON, D. and PARLETT, M. (1972) 'Evaluation as illumination', Occasional Paper, No. 9, Centre for Research in Educational Studies, Edinburgh University.

HAMILTON, D. (1976) *Curriculum Evaluation*, Open Books.

HAMMERSLEY, M. and WOODS, P. (1976) *The Process of Schooling*, Open University Press.

HARGREAVES, D. H. (1972) *Interpersonal Relations and Education*, RKP.

HARGREAVES, D. H. (1978) 'Deviance: the interactionist approach', in GILLHAM, B. (ed.) *Reconstructing Educational Psychology*, Croom Helm: London.

HARRIS, J. (1978) 'Primacy, the child psychiatric clinic and the educational psychologist', AEP *Journal*, Vol. 4, No. 7, pp. 49—52.

HAZELL, J. (1973). 'Describing Depersonalization', *British Journal of Guidance and Counselling*, Vol. 1, No. 1, pp. 17—28.

HEARNSHAW, L. S. (1964) *A Short History of British Psychology*, Methuen.

HENRY, J. (1955) 'Docility or giving teacher what she wants', *Journal of Social Issues*, Vol. 11, pp. 33—41.

HENRY, J. (1966) *Culture Against Man*, Tavistock.

HERAUD, B. J. (1970) *Sociology and Social Work*, Pergamon International Library.

HERITAGE, J. (1974) 'Assessing People', in ARMISTEAD, N. (ed.) *Reconstructing Social Psychology*, Penguin Education.

HOLLY, D. (1972) *Society, Schools and Humanity*, Paladin.

HOLT, J. (1964). *How Children Fail*, Pitman; 1969, Penguin.

HOLT, J. (1967) *How Children Learn*, Penguin.

HOPSON, B. and HOUGH, P. (1976) 'The need for personal and social education in secondary schools and further education', *British Journal of Guidance and Counselling*, Vol. 4, No. 1, pp. 16—27.

INGLEBY, D. (1974) 'The psychology of child psychology' in RICHARDS, M. P. M. *"The Integration of a Child into a Social World"*, pp. 295—308, Cambridge University Press.

INGLEBY, D. (1974) 'The job psychologists do' in ARMISTEAD, N. (ed.) *Reconstructing Social Psychology*, Penguin.

JACOBY, R. (1975) *Social Amnesia: A Critique of Conformist Psychology from Adler to Laing*, Boston: Beacon Press.

JAMES, C. (1964) 'Keeping open the door of opportunity', *Journal and Newsletter* of the AEP, No. 1, September.

JAMES, C. (1970) 'Modern concepts of intelligence', *Journal and Newsletter* of the AEP, Vol. 2, No. 5, Spring.

KAMIN, L. J. (1974) *The Science and Politics of IQ*, Lawrence Erlbaum Associates, Penguin, 1977.

KARIER, C. (1976) 'Testing for order and control in the corporate liberal state', in DALE, R. *et al.*, *Schooling and Capitalism*, RKP, Open University Course Reader, Reading 14.

KEIR, G. (1952) 'Symposium on psychologists and psychiatrists in Child Guidance Services', *British Journal of Educational Psychology*, Vol. 22, pp. 5—29.

KELLY, G. A. (1955) *The Psychology of Personal Constructs*, New York: Norton.

KUHN, T. S. (1962) *The Structure of Scientific Revolutions*, University of Chicago Press.

LABOV, W. (1973) 'The logic of non standard English', in KEDDIE, N. (ed.) *Tinker, Tailor... the Myth of Cultural Deprivation*, Hamondsworth, Penguin.

LARSON, R. S. (1977) *The Rise of Professionalism, A Sociological Analysis*, University of California Press.

LEACH, D. J. and RAYBOULD, E. C. (1977) *Learning and Behaviour Difficulties in School*, Open Books, London.

LEONARD, P. (1975) 'A Paradigm for Radical Practice', in BAILEY, R. and BRAKE, M. *Radical Social Work*, Edward Arnold.

LONDON, P. (1972) 'The end of ideology in behaviour modification, *American Psychologist*, 27, pp. 913—920.

LOVE, P. (1977) 'Educational psychology and the Court Report', AEP *Journal* Vol. 4, No. 5, pp. 2—6. Presidential Address given at the 1977 Conference of the Association.

LUKES, S. (1977) *Essays in Social Theory*, The MacMillan Press Ltd.

MACDONALD-ROSS, M. (1973) 'Behavioural Objectives — A Critical Review', *Instructional Science*, May.

MAGER, R. F. (1975) *Preparing Instructional Objectives*, Belmont, California, Fearon.

MASLOW, A. (1956) 'Self actualizing people: a study of psychological growth', in MOUSTAKAS, C. E. (ed.) *The Self: Explorations in Personal Growth*, New York, Harper and Row.

MEACHAM, M. L. and WIESEN, A. E. (1969) *Changing Classroom Behaviour*, Scranton, International Text Book Co.

MOODY, R. L. (1952) 'Symposium of psychologists and psychiatrists in Child Guidance Services V — A conflict of disciplines and personalities', *British Journal of Educational Psychology*, Vol. 22, November, pp. 155—9.

MORRIS, R. (1963) *Success and Failure in Learning to Read*, Penguin.

PATTERSON, C. H. (1974) 'Humanistic education: the challenge to the counsellor', *British Journal of Guidance and Counselling*, Vol. 2, No. 1, pp. 2—14.

PEARSON, L. (1975) 'Developmental scales in the British Intelligence Scale', Paper presented to the Annual Conference of the British Psychological Society, 4 April, 1975.

PERROW, C. (1979) *Complex Organizations*, Scott Foresman and Company, Illinois.

PETTIGREW, A. M. (1973) 'Occupational specialisation as an emergent process', *Sociological Review*, Vol. 2, p. 259.

PHILLIPS, C. J. (1974) 'Questionnaire on Training', Occasional Papers of the Division of Educational and Child Psychology of the British Psychological Society, No. 5, Spring.

PHILLIPS, D. C. and KELLY, M. E. (1975) 'Hierarchical theories of development in education and psychology', *Harvard Education Review*, 45, pp. 351—375.

PLATT, A. M. (1969) *The Child Savers: The Invention of Delinquency*, University of Chicago Press.

Plowden Report (1967) *Children and their Primary Schools*, Central Advisory Council for Education (England), London, HMSO.

PRESLAND, J. (1970) 'Who should go to ESN schools?' *Special Education*, Vol. 59, No. 1, pp. 11—17.

PRESLAND, J. (1972) 'Helping the maladjusted child', AEP *Journal*, Vol. 3, No. 2, pp. 31—40.

PRESLAND, J. (1976) Reply to J. C. Quicke, AEP *Journal*, Vol. 4, No. 1, p. 52.

PRESLAND, J. and ROE, M. (1978) 'Monitoring, assessment and the L.E.A. psychologist', AEP *Journal*, Vol. 4, No. 8, pp. 20—28.

Psychiatry Section of the Royal Society of Medicine debate on the 'Difficult Child', *Lancet* (1929) 2, 1251—3.

QUICKE, J. C. (1977) 'The psychologist and educational research', AEP *Journal*, Vol. 4, No. 4, pp. 8—11.

RAVENETTE, A. T. (1968) *Dimensions of Reading Difficulties*, Pergamon Press.

RAVENETTE, A. T. (1972) 'Maladjustment, clinical concept and administrative convenience. Psychologists, teachers and children. How many ways to understand?', AEP *Journal*, Vol. 3, No. 3, pp. 41—7.

RAVENETTE, A. T. (1974) 'Intelligence and Intelligence Testing', AEP *Journal*, Vol. 3, No. 6, pp. 15—17.

RAVENETTE, A. T. (1974) 'Presidential Encyclical', AEP *Journal*, Vol. 3, No. 7, pp. 1—4.

REID, R. S. (1965) Editorial, 'Psychologists, psychiatrists and child guidance', *Journal and Newsletter* of the Association of Educational Psychologists, No. 4, page 3.

REID, R. S. (1978) 'Am I right in thinking — drums in the jungle', AEP *Journal*, Vol. 4, No. 8, pp. 47—50.

RICHARDSON, E. (1973) *The Teacher, the School and the Task of Management*, London, Heinemann.

ROBB, G. (1968) in the *Journal and Newsletter* of the AEP, Vol. 2, No. 3, p. 32.

ROE, M. (1964) 'Creating a viable ambiance', *Newsletter* of the AEP, No. 1.

ROE, M. (1978) 'Medical and psychological concepts of problem behaviour', in GILLHAM, B. (ed.) *Reconstructing Educational Psychology*, Croom Helm, London.

ROGERS, C. R. (1942) *Counselling and Psychotherapy*, Boston, Houghton Mifflin.

ROGERS, C. R. (1951) *Client-centred Therapy*, Houghton Mifflin.

ROGERS, C. R. (1965) 'The therapeutic relationship: recent theory and research', *Australian Journal of Psychology*, Vol. 17, No. 2, pp. 95—108.

ROGERS, C. R. (1969) *Freedom to Learn*, Merrill.

ROSEN, H. (1965) *Lanugage and Literacy in our Schools: Some Appraisals of the Bullock Report*, National Foundation for Educational Research.

ROTH, D. (1974) 'Intelligence testing as a social activity' in CICOUREL et al *Language Use and School Performance*, Academic Press.

SAMPSON, O. (1980) 'Child guidance: its history, provenance and future', Occasional Papers of the Division of Educational and Child Psychology, British Psychological Society, Vol. 3, No. 3.

SCHUR, E. (1976) *The Awareness Trap: Self Absorption instead of Social Change*, New York: Quadrangle/The New York Times Book Co.

SHEARER, A, (1981) *Disability: Whose Handicap?*, Basil Blackwell.

SIMON, B. (1974) *The Politics of Educational Reform — 1920—1940*, Lawrence and Wishart.

SKINNER, B. F. (1974) 'Designing Higher Education', *Daedelus*, 1, pp. 196—202.

STAATS, A. W. and BUTTERFIELD, W. H. (1965) 'Treatment of non-reading in a culturally deprived juvenile delinquent: an application of reinforcement principles', *Child Development*, Vol. 36, No. 4, December, pp. 925—942.

STATHAM, D. (1978) *Radicals in Social Work*, Routledge and Kegan Paul.

STEWART, W. A. C. (1972) *Progressives and Radicals in English Education*, MacMillan.

SUMMERFIELD, A. et al. (1968) *Psychologists in Education Services*, HMSO.

SUTHERLAND, G. (1981) 'The Origins of Special Education', in SWANN, W. (ed.) *The Practice of Special Education*, Basil Blackwell in association with the Open University Press.

SUTTON, A. (1978) 'The psychologist's professionalism and the right to psychology' in GILLHAM, B. (ed.) *Reconstructing Educational Psychology*, Croom Helm.

SWIFT, D. F. (1973) 'Sociology and Educational Research' in TAYLOR, W. *Research Perspectives in Education*, Routledge and Kegan Paul.

TAYLOR, I., WALTON, P. and YOUNG, J. (1975) 'Critical criminology in Britain: review and prospects' in TAYLOR, I. et al. *Critical Criminology*, Routlege and Kegan Paul.

TAYLOR, M. T. (1976) 'What is a personal construct?' *Psychology Teaching*, Vol. 4, No. 2, November.

TAYLOR, W. (1968) *Half a Million Teachers*, Bristol University, Institute of Education.

TERMAN, L. M. and MERRILL, M. A. (1937) *Measuring Intelligence*, London, Harrap.

TIBBLE, J. W. in the *Journal of Educational Studies*, No. 10, 1961–2, p. 68.

TIZARD, J. (1976) 'Psychology and social policy', *Bulletin* of the British Psychological Society, 29, pp. 225–234.

TOMLINSON, S. (1981) *Education Subnormality: A Study in Decision-Making*, Routledge and Kegan Paul.

Underwood Report, *Report of the Committee on Maladjusted Children*, (1955), London, HMSO.

VALETT, R. E. (1963) *The Practice of School Psychology, Professional Problems*, New York, Wiley.

VERNON, P. E. (1950) *Modern Educational Psychology as a Science*, Evans Brothers for the University of London Institute of Education.

VERNON, P. E. (1970) 'Development of current ideas about intelligence tests', in JAMES, C., *op. cit.*

WALL, W. D. (1956) *Psychological Services for Schools* UNESCO Institute for Education, Hamburg.

Warnock Report (1978) *Report of the Committee of Enquiry into the Education of Handicapped Children and Young People*, London, HMSO.

WILLIAMS, P. in CHAZAN *et al* (1974) *op. cit.*

WOLFENDALE, S. (1976) 'Screening and early identification of reading and learning difficulties — a description of the Croydon screening procedures', in WEDELL, K. and RAYBOULD, E. C. *The Early Identification of Educationally 'At Risk' Children*, University of Birmingham.

The Wood Committee, Board of Education and Board of Control (1929) *Report of the Joint Departmental Committee on Mental Deficiency*, London, HMSO.

WOODS, P. (1980) *Pupil Strategies*, Croom Helm.

WOODY, R. H. (1968) 'British behavioural counselling', *Educational Research*, 10, pp. 209–212.

WRIGHT, H. J. (1975) 'Presidential Encyclical' in AEP *Journal*, Vol. 3, No. 9 (insert).

WRIGHT, H. J. and PAYNE, T. A. N. (1979) *An Evaluation of a School Psychological Service — The Portsmouth Pattern*, Published by the Hampshire County Council.

WRIGHT MILLS, C. (1942) 'The professional ideology of social pathologists', *American Journal of Sociology*, 49, (Sept.) pp. 165–180.

YOUNG, J. (1979) 'Left idealism, reformism and beyond: from new criminology to Marxism' in *Capitalism and the Rule of Law*, Editorial Collective, Hutchinson of London.

Unpublished documents

Association of Educational Psychologists:

- AEP/14/75 'Assessment of the special educational needs of handicapped pupils' — Circular 2/75, 26 June 1975.
- Resume of informal meeting of the Department of Education and Science, 6 February 1976.
- Copy letter for information to professor Hetherington — working party on child psychologists, 30 June 1976.
- AEP/5/77: 'Psychologists in the Health Service', 18 February 1977.
- AEP/20/77: 'Commentary on *Fit for the Future*' 15 June 1977.
- Circular 2/75 Review of Forms SE 1–6, 12 August 1977.
- 'Comments on *The Role of Psychologists in Health Services* — The Report of the Trethowan Committee', 16 August 1977.
- AEP/10/78: Resolutions of the 1978 Annual General Meeting requiring action by the Executive Committee, 13 April 1978.
- Association of Educational Psychologists: 'Special educational needs — comments on the consultative document on the *Report of the the Committee of Enquiry into the Education of Handicapped and Young People*', 11 December 1978.

Index

Adams, Sir John, 4, 6
Ainscow, M., 107, 108
Alexander, Sir William, 26
alienation, 140
alternatives, 60, 122–149
Association of Educational Psychologists, 25–27, 28–37, 106
'awareness craze', 97, 98

Ballard, P. B., 3
Banks, C., 22
Bannon, W. J., 26
Becker, W., 110
behavioural approach, 106–121, 144; appeal of, 110–112; application to education, 106; behavioural deviance, 115–117; behavioural objectives, 107–109, 112–115; behaviour modification, 109–110, 115–120; and 'crude' behaviourism, 107; and the curriculum, 113–115; humanistic behaviourism, 118; the 'medical model', compared with, 111; mystification as an example of, 144; radical claims of, 112, 120; and reading, 113; and self, 119.
behavioural objectives (*see* behavioural approach)
behaviourism, 5, 64, 74, 75 (*see also* behavioural approach)
behaviour modification (*see* behavioural approach)

Bell, D., 144
Berger, P. L., 96
Bernstein, B., 66
Bersoff, D. N., 83
Binet, A., 17, 18, 46
biology, 2, 3, 55, 56, 76, 97, 125
Bitensky, R., 52
Blackham, G. J., 118
blind, 10, 11, 12
Blumer, H., 127
Board of Education, 7, 15
Booth, Tony, 122
Bowlby, J., 66
British Ability Scales, 43–48, 52, 61
British Child Study Association, 14
British Journal of Educational Psychology, 3, 22, 65, 68
British Journal of Sociology, 68
British Psychological Society, 25
BPS Bulletin, 65, 68
Bruner, J., 9, 140
Bullock Report, 116
Burden, R., 123, 125, 127
bureaucracy, 74
Burns, R., 106
Burt, C., 2, 6, 8, 12, 15, 17, 18, 22, 45, 46, 105
Butterfield, W., 113

Cambridge University, 4, 6
'capacity model', 44
caring school, 81

case work (*see* ideology)
cautious expert, 57–58
Chazan, M., 42, 115
child centred education, 9
Child Guidance Clinic, 14–17, 21–23, 27, 33
Child Guidance Service, 22, 23, 26, 30
child psychologist, 30, 31
Child Study Movement, 4, 14
Circular 2/75, 29, 35
Circular 3/74, 30, 35
Claparède, E., 18
class conflict, 139
client-centred therapy, 99
clinical medical officers, 38, 42
clinical psychologists, 30, 32, 33, 34
cognitive, 64, 87
Cohen, S., 141–147
'coming of age', 29–31
Committee on Defective and Epileptic Children, 11
common sense knowledge, 74, 76
competitive society, 102
constructs (*see* personal constructs)
contradiction, 71, 76
Cooke, C. T., 42
counselling, 98, 118
Court Report, 31–35, 36, 37, 67
Crabtree, T. W., 28
Cronbach, L. J., 114
Croydon Check List, 116, 117
culture, 49–52, 128, 137
curriculum: evaluation, 134–136; innovation, 131; hidden curriculum, 129; and traditional tests, 48; (*see also* culture)

Dale, R., 125
Davidson, M., 21
deaf, 12, 13
democratic attitude, 147, 148
demystification, 144, 145
Dent, H. C., 4
Department of Education and Science, 29, 30
depersonalization, 102, 119, 120
deschooling, 139

Dessent, T., 110, 111
Dewey, J., 9, 65
developmental perspective, 64
deviance, 66, 119, 120, 128, 132, 134, 140, 143–144
disability, 137
District Handicap Teams, 35, 36
Division of Education and Child Psychology (of the BPS), 131
Donaldson, M., 48

eclecticism, 64, 141, 142
Education Acts: (1870) 10; (1899) 11; (1944) 12, 16, 25, 27
educational psychology: application to education, 3, 4; establishment of, 1–19; 'new psychology', 2, 3; and radical education, 8–10; role in education, 5–10 (*see also* traditional practitioner paradigm; psychometrics; educational psychologists)
educational psychologists: and advisory service, 37; attitudes to esoteric knowledge, 74–80; attitudes to research, 68–70; attitudes to schools, 80–82; attitudes to tests, 70–74; 'coming of age', 29–31; diagnosis and treatment of handicapped children, 13; differences from psychiatrists, 16, 21; early psychologists, 15; early role in Europe and America, 18, 19; expert role, 57, 58; first official post, 17; Government reports, 27, 28, 29, 31–36; identity, 1, 53; a 'new' profession, 20; perspectives, 63–65; professional association, 25–26; professional struggles, 20–39; professional survival, 52–53; as a radical change agent, 140–149; reading, 66–67; and special education, 12, 29, 30, 35, 36; use of tests, 61–63; (*see also* Child Guidance; School Psychological Service; Association of Educational Psychologists; Summerfield,

Court, Trethowan, Warnock Reports; education psychology; traditional practitioner paradigm)
educational research, 68–70
Educational Research (Journal), 68
educational subnormality, 13, 28
Egerton Commission, 10
Elliot, C., 43, 44, 45, 46, 67
Elliot, P., 52
encroachment, 21, 34
English teachers, 113
Entwistle, H., 50
epileptic, 13
evaluation (see curriculum)
expertism, 20, 57, 77
exploratory approach, 94–96, 114

Fabian, 20
facilitator, 101
First World War, 12
Fisher, R. A., 6
Freeman, A., 42
Freud, S., 9

Galloway, D., 125
George, V., 20, 139
Giddens, A., 54
Gillham, W., 49, 51, 52
Grace, G., 139
Graham, C., 45
Green, A., 99
Grid Technique (see personal constructs)
Guntrip, H., 102

Hadow Report, 6, 7
Hamilton, D., 135
Hammersley, M., 135
Handicapped Pupils and School Health Service Regulations (1945), 13
Hargreaves, D., 66, 110, 131–133
Hazell, J., 102
Hearnshaw, L. S., 3, 8
'helping profession', 80
Henry, J., 101
Heraud, B. J., 1
Heritage, J., 99

Hester Adrian Centre, 67
Hetherington, Professor, 31
hidden curriculum (see curriculum)
historical materialism, 64
Holly, D., 140
Holt, J., 51, 140
Homer Lane, 8
Hopson, B., 98
Hough, P., 98
HP (Handicapped Pupils), Forms, 29

identity crisis, 103
ideology, 139; of case work, 142, 144
illuminative evaluation, 135
individualism (see methodological individualism)
Ingleby, D., 20
in-service training, 132–134
institutional level, 125
Institutes of Education, 6, 9
integration, 147
intelligence tests, 13, 14, 40ff, 61, 62 (see also educational psychologists, psychometrics)
interactionist perspective: defined, 127–129; implications for practice, 129–136; symbolic interactionism, 127; (see also labelling; in-service training; curriculum)
intervention, point of, 115–117, 121
invalidation, 120
Isaacs, S., 9, 105

Jacoby, R., 103
James, C., 45
Jewish Health Organization, 15
Journal and Newsletter (AEP), 27, 28, 33, 34–45; AEP Journal, 68
Journal of Experimental Pedagogy, 3
Journal of Statistical Psychology, 6

Kamin, L. J., 47
Karier, C., 55
Kelly, G., 75, 86–96 (see non-directive style; personal constructs)

Kimmins, C. W., 3
knowledge base (*see* educational psychologists)
Kohlbergh, L., 55, 56
Kuhn, T. S., 54

labelling, 85, 112, 120, 121, 128, 129, 137, 143 (*see also* interactionist perspective)
Labov, W., 50
Larson, R. S., 53
'latent traits', 43, 45
Leach, D. J., 67, 106, 104, 115, 119, 120
Leonard, P., 142
liberal ideology (*see* ideology)
local education authority, 25, 37, 38
London County Council (London School Board), 3, 11, 15, 17
London Day Training College, 4
London, P., 144
Love, P., 33, 35
Lukes, S., 55, 56

MacDonald Ross, M., 114
McDougall, W., 2, 3, 4
McKenzie, M. G., 113
MacMillan, R., 8
'macro', 52, 136, 137
Mager, R. F., 107, 112
maladjustment, 13, 22, 94, 106, 111, 147
Maslow, A., 103
Mathiesen, T., 145
Meacham, M. L., 118
Medical Officer of Health, 28
medical model, 84, 112, 149
Mental Deficiency Act (1913), 11
Merrill, M., 46
methodological individualism, 55-57
Mittler, P., 67
Montessori, M., 8, 9
Moodie, Dr., 15
Moody, R. L., 23
Morant, Sir Robert, 7
Morris, R., 113

multi-disciplinary teams, 38 (*see also* Child Guidance)
Myers, C. S., 4

National Health Service, 34
National Union of Teachers, 32
Neale Analysis of Reading Ability, 61
negative labelling, 120-121 (*see also* labelling)
negotiation, 116, 128, 129, 148
'new' psychology, 2, 3, 9
non-directiveness, 78, 79, 80, 84; style, 86-105; diagnosis and treatment, 98, 99, 100; and change in schools, 101; paradox of, 101-104 (*see also* personal constructs)
non-referral basis, 142
normalization, 130
norm referenced tests, 62, 63
Norwood Report, 7
Nunn, P., 2, 4, 9

objectives, behavioural (*see* behavioural approach)
'old' psychology, 2
operationalism, 114
oppression, 117, 140, 143, 148
order model, 137, 138, 139
Oxford, 4

paradigm (*see* traditional practitioner paradigm)
Parlett, M., 135
Patterson, C. H. 102
Payne, T. A. N., 38
Pearson, L., 43
Peel, E. A., 5
Perrow, C., 124
personal constructs, 88-96; defined, 89-90; criticisms of, 95-96; Repertory Grid Technique, 91-94; use in school context, 94-95
perspectives, 63-65
Pettigrew, A. M., 52
phenomenological, 51, 87
Phillips, C. J., 42

Phillips, D. C., 48
physically handicapped, 13
Piaget, J., 48, 55, 65, 66
Platt, A., 16
Plowden Report, 44, 52
positivism, 83, 114
Presland, J., 40, 107, 111
psychiatrist, 16, 17, 21-23, 35, 38
progressive education, 9
psychology, 5, 6 (*see* educational psychology)
psychometrics, 6, 7, 40-53, 61-63

questionnaire study, 59-70
Quicke, J. C., 141

radical change, 84, 140
radical education, 8-10
radical practice, 141
Ravenette, A. T., 30, 31, 51, 86, 94, 95
Raybould, E. L., 67, 106, 109, 116, 119, 120
'realness', 97
reconstructing, 96, 110, 111
reflective role, 79, 98
Regional Health Authority, 38
Reid, R. S., 34
reification, 71
remedial education, 37
Remedial Education Centre, 37
Repertory Grid Technique (*see* personal constructs)
research (*see* educational research)
Richardson, E., 126
Robb, G., 27
Roe, M., 111
Rogers, C., 74, 75, 86, 87, 88, 97-104 (*see also* non-directive style)
Rosen, H., 113
Roth, D., 51
rules, 128, 129, 132, 133
Rupiper, O. J., 106
Rusk, R., 2, 4, 6

Sampson, O., 14
Schonell, F. J., 5, 37, 61

School Psychological Service, 17-19, 24-25, 29, 148
Schur, E., 97
self actualizing tendency, 97, 98
self directed change, 100, 101
self theory, 103
Shearer, A., 137
Silberman, A., 118
Simon, B., 7, 8
Skinner, B. F., 65, 106, 113, 117
social psychology, 4
Social Services, 38
Society of Education Officers, 32
sociological orientation, 123-140
sociology, 56, 64, 67
Spearman, 6
special education, 10-14, 25, 30, 36, 61, 146, 147
speech defective, 13
Staats, A. W., 113
Stanford Binet, 28, 62
Statham, D., 141
Stewart, W. A. C., 4
Stern, W., 18
stigma, 129
streaming, 7
structural analysis, 56
structural functionalist, 139
subjectivity, 91-94
Sully, J., 2, 3, 15
Summerfield Report, 26, 27, 28
Sutherland, G., 10
Swift, D. F., 52
symbolic interactionism (*see* interactionism)
'systems' approach, 123-127, 138

Tansley, A. E., 65
Taylor, I., 20
Taylor, M. T., 93
Taylor, W., 83
Terman, L. M., 46, 47
testing (*see* intelligence tests; psychometrics)
theory, 67, 75
Thomson, G., 5, 6
Tibble, J. W., 4
Times Educational Supplement, 68

Tizard, J., 111
Tomlinson, S., 11
Topping, J. K., 42
traditional practitioner paradigm, 54–57
training (*see* in-service training)
Trethowan Report, 31–35
Tweddle, D., 107, 112
typifications, 96, 129, 137

Underwood Report, 21, 23, 27
UNESCO, 24

Valentine, C. W., 5, 6
Valett, R. E., 1
Vernon, P. E., 45, 46, 57

Wall, W. D., 2, 19, 24, 37, 38

Walton, P., 20
Ward, James, 2
Warnock Report, 35, 36, 136
Wechsler Intelligence Scale for Children, 44, 61, 62, 72
Wiesen, M. L., 118
Wilding, P., 20, 139
Williams, P., 23, 29
Winch, W. H., 3
Wolfendale, S., 116
Wolpe, J., 11
Wood Committee, 13
Woods, P., 135
Woody, R. H., 106, 118
Wright, H. J., 29, 38
Wright Mills, C., 141

Young, J., 20, 140